An Ordinary Life

To Lee & Emmy Lou
With warmest thanks for
many happy memories
with our oldest friends
                    Bob

An Ordinary Life

A Memoir

Robert F. Patton

To Lee & Cherry Lou
With thanks for
fond memories
Bob

iUniverse, Inc.
New York Lincoln Shanghai

An Ordinary Life

Copyright © 2006 by Robert F. Patton

iUniverse books may be ordered through booksellers or by contacting:

iUniverse
2021 Pine Lake Road, Suite 100
Lincoln, NE 68512
www.iuniverse.com
1-800-Authors (1-800-288-4677)

ISBN-13: 978-0-595-38598-0 (pbk)
ISBN-13: 978-0-595-82979-8 (ebk)
ISBN-10: 0-595-38598-2 (pbk)
ISBN-10: 0-595-82979-1 (ebk)

Printed in the United States of America

Contents

Foreword

Perhaps one should apologize for writing a book, especially one so egocentric as an autobiography. This will have to do. The inspiration for this opus goes back many years to a book written about my great-grandfather, a man by the name of Isaac P. Rose. The book is entitled *"Four Years in the Rockies"* and is available in some libraries such as the Carnegie here in Pittsburgh. It is the story of his four years in the 1830s when he was a trapper with Jim Bridger's company, and contains many tales of people like Kit Carson, the fierce Indians and the mountain men of that time. After his youthful adventures, he came back to New Castle and became a teacher, a farmer and a local magistrate, but he never wrote anything about his ordinary life. I would like to have known about that as well, and it seemed to me that stories about one's ordinary life might be interesting to future generations of the writer.

I missed the Great Adventure of my time, World War II, by reason of my date of birth. So I have no stories of heroism, battle scenes and the like. I have just led an ordinary life like most people, but it is a life I have enjoyed and I would like to tell you about it.

1

Early On

When you hold an infant in your arms, do you ever wonder what that child's life will be like? Will it be a long, productive and happy life or the opposite? It's impossible to tell, is it not? The child's genetic inheritance, the influence of its parents, teachers, family and everyone it meets will change that life. Wars, epidemics or accidents may end it prematurely. The best you can do is offer up a prayer, wish it the best and hope to be one of the positive influences on that life. Someone may have done that for me, which leads me to the story of my life and the people and events that shaped it.

According to usually reliable witnesses, I was born on December 9, 1927, at the home of my parents, Wylie and Lena Patton, in Hickory Township, Lawrence County, Pennsylvania. When I first got a birth certificate, maybe thirty years later, I discovered that the Bureau of Vital Statistics of this Commonwealth was under the impression I had been born on December 11. After some discussion and an affidavit from my parents, they obligingly agreed to change their records to the 9th. My mother's theory was that the doctor had been busy and hadn't gotten around to preparing a birth certificate until a month later, and he was confused about the date. So much for the infallibility of public records.

Otherwise, that Friday didn't seem like much of a day for news. The excitement of the crash of 1929 and the Great Depression were still ahead of us. The big social and political issue of that day was Prohibition. The New York Herald Tribune on December 9 (given to me as a birthday present on my 60th birthday) reported that Mr. Kresge of the five-and-dime stores had arisen at a dinner of the Anti-Saloon League and pledged a half million dollars to their $10 million dollar fund to be used for prohibition propaganda. The Commander of the American Legion announced that it would conduct a poll of its membership in the spring on "the prohibition question". The sagging springs of a car tipped off the New

1

Jersey police to investigate, thereby finding the woman driver had 26 cases of booze in the rumble seat (if you don't know the cars of that era, you may not know what a rumble seat is). I, of course, had been born into a "dry" household, but was willing to hear from both sides.

In other news, Charles Lindbergh announced that he would make one last flight on the "Spirit of St. Louis" to Mexico City before placing it in the Smithsonian. Perhaps the most timeless news of the day was the account of an address by Dr. Edward Steiner, professor of sociology at Grinnell University, in which he asserted that education in this country was creating snobbishness among those educated which was more destructive than ignorance. He had other opinions as well, including the thought that the "100 percent American" was as mischievous as *"Deutschland uber Alles"*. Among distinguished guests listening to this academic twaddle were Conde Nast, Walter Damrosch and the Reverend Harry Fosdick.

So it wasn't a big news day, but I didn't care, I had arrived. Of course, I didn't realize how lucky I had been: born in the United States, with loving parents, being raised on a farm, with an older brother (and after four years, a younger brother). I had to travel over a good bit of the world as an adult to understand that on the day I was born I had won the lottery!

My parents were lifelong residents of Lawrence County, and except for my father's Army service in France and Germany in the Great War, had never lived away from there. He had gone to Penn State for two years before his military service. Dad was the fifth generation of Pattons to have lived in Hickory Township, where our immigrant ancestor, William Patton, had been one of the first settlers in 1800. He and some fellow immigrants from Ireland had bought a tract of land from a major in the Revolutionary War, who had received it as part of the Donation Lands distributed to veterans of that war.

My mother's parents, Edward and Olive Gardner, also lived in Hickory Township, about a mile from my grandfather Patton's farm, and the two grandfathers had been close friends. It must have made them happy to see their children marry, but, alas, I could never ask them, as both died before or shortly after I was born. The same for my grandmother Gardner, so the only grandparent I ever knew was my Grandma Patton. She was a quiet, sweet-tempered little old lady who lived to her 88th year, when I was in my twenties. She had produced seven children, including my father, another son (my Uncle Tom), and five daughters, five of the best aunts one could have selected.

Grandma Patton's source of support was the farm (they hadn't invented Social Security yet), and my father was the designated hitter to farm it. He did not have an easy life, as he had a full-time job as a rural mail carrier and later as a supervisor in the New Castle Post Office. He must have been grateful for three sons, since after a few years we could help with the farm chores. It was about a sixty-acre farm, a mile East of New Castle on the Harlansburg Road (Rt. 108). Cash income came from milk, and there were usually about a dozen head of cows, accompanied by a bull until they discovered artificial insemination.

Dad was six feet tall and was all muscle and bone. At my best, I was never as strong as he was. He was quiet and even-tempered, and most people liked him. I never heard anybody call him anything but "Wylie". He smoked a pipe, in the house, but in the barn and outdoors he chewed Mail Pouch tobacco. My mother was six or seven inches shorter and stout. She had a quick temper and it was best not to cross her, but she enjoyed a joke and had a hearty laugh.

It is hard to imagine a more confining life than a dairy farm. The cows have to be milked twice a day, every day of the year, rain or shine. There were no hired hands, so there never was a day of vacation. Until about the time I was seven or so, there were horses to help with the plowing, harvesting and general work of the farm. They were replaced by a 1935 John Deere tractor, a marvel of engineering simplicity, which operated until Dad died, and since then has been restored by a neighboring farmer and is shown as an antique at farm shows. My brother Willard cried when the horses were led away, I suppose to the glue factory, but I hadn't formed any attachment to them.

The earliest clear memory I have of my childhood was the day in January of 1931 when my younger brother, Gaylord, was born. Willard, (he was five and I was four) and I knew something exciting was afoot, as we were packed off in the Winter morning darkness to Grandma Patton's house, just up the road. We played there until early afternoon, when we were taken home to greet our new brother. I was reported to have asked the perceptive question "Where did *he* come from?" As the displaced baby of the family, I probably was thinking "and who invited him?" But from then on, I had the position of "middle child".

It is hard to sort out my early memories from those of later years, as we lived in the same place throughout, and the seasons passed with a familiar regularity, making it difficult to distinguish one year from another. I remember the Christmas when we boys got our first dog, a fine liver-and-white Springer Spaniel pup with big feet especially designed for tracking mud into the house and front porch. We named him "Dandy", and he was. I must have been about five.

I also remember my first movie, which was "Black Beauty", and I would guess that I was then about five years old. It was in black-and-white, but it had sound. Talking movies were the latest thing, and my mother took Willard and me into the movie house on East Washington Street in New Castle to see it. I thought the cartoons before the movie were hilarious, and Mom said I laughed louder than anyone in the theater. I probably never again enjoyed any movie as much as that one; the whole business seemed miraculous, which would be hard for anyone raised in the era of television to understand.

We also got our first radio about that time, and this was a momentous purchase for the whole family. Dad had two big consoles brought into the house, we listened to both of them and debated their merits, and we each expressed our preference. I don't know that a majority vote won, but we bought one of them, and it was the major source of family entertainment as we grew up. The radio programs were just great: *"Tom Mix"; "The Lone Ranger"; "Jack Armstrong, the All American Boy"*, with secret decoder rings; *"Little Orphan Annie"; "Inner Sanctum"*, and every Sunday evening we laughed with Jack Benny. For those of you who can't remember pre-television days, that medium didn't arrive until about twenty years later, and you missed a lot in the radio shows of the 30's.

Through all my childhood, I had the nice sense of being part of an extended family, at least on my father's side. With six sets of aunts and uncles on my Dad's side, and eighteen cousins, we did not lack for family on holidays. Grandma Patton's house, just up the road from us, was the usual holiday gathering place, and some would come for several weeks in the summer for a farm vacation. I was about in the middle of the pack in age, and there were seven or eight of us within a year or two of my age.

I wasn't so well endowed with relatives on my mother's side. She had one sister, Vera Patton, married to a second cousin of Dad's named Norman Patton. They had one daughter, Evelyn Francis, who contracted polio and died when she was about eleven years old. I must have been about four at the time, and have only a dim recollection of that cousin. Vera was about six years older than Mother, and the two of them argued and quarreled like siblings as long as Vera lived.

I was called "Robby" in those days. When I got a little older and went to school, my contemporaries called me "Bob", as I guess they thought "Robby" was insultingly diminutive. But my parents and people of their generation called me "Robby" for some years, and when they thought it was *infra dig.*, changed it to "Robert". But my Dad called me "Robby" until the day he died, and I rather liked it: it was a link to my childhood, and perhaps I felt he was patting me on my head when he said it.

What was it like living there at that time? Well, the day of the horse and buggy had passed during my parents' lifetime, and the roads were paved, or at least most of them. Many of the country roads were called "Pinchot roads" for the Governor who had started the program for paving the dirt roads of Pennsylvania. We had indoor plumbing at our house, but Grandma did not, having an outhouse behind the barn at her house for most of those years. The cars driven were those marvelous 1930's models, which still seem to me to be the best that Detroit ever made. Airplanes were still in their infancy (I had just missed Lindy's great flight), and I was never on one until I was in the Army. Train travel was the prevailing mode for long distance travel, and the Pennsylvania Railroad was still a great financial power. My Uncle Carl Sewall, married to Dad's sister Nancy, worked for the Pennsy, and he had the rare privilege of traveling free. So the Sewall family, with three girls close to my age, who lived in Altoona and later in Philadelphia, came often to visit Grandma Patton.

When I was still quite young, four or five, my mother took Willard and me on a train trip to Philadelphia and Atlantic City, visiting the Sewalls on the way, and that was a big adventure but I don't remember much about it. The purpose of the trip, according to my mother, was to show us what a train trip was like, and I do remember the great Horseshoe Curve near Altoona, and going to the Sewall's apartment.

All in all, I was lucky to have all of the elements making for a happy childhood, and that's the way I remember it.

2

Growin' Up

To start with, it's fun to grow up with two brothers. We weren't any better than the usual run of boys, we played a lot, fought a lot, and drove my mother to despair more than once. Willard was my older brother, but only fifteen months older, so we went through school just one grade apart. But he was bigger and stronger, and there wasn't any doubt who the junior was. He was always loquacious and extroverted, leaving me with the role of the shy and quiet younger brother. When he was an adult, old-timers who could remember said he was the personification of his grandfather, Ed Gardner. He was dark-haired and I was blond. I was clearly a Patton. Gaylord was four years younger, and therefore in a younger generation as far as Willard and I were concerned. He looked more like me.

Our parents took us to church every Sunday at Neshannock United Presbyterian Church, about a mile from our house. The church property, including the cemetery, had been donated by our ancestor, William Patton and his son Archibald, who were among the founding members of that congregation. All of the Pattons since then are buried there, and you can get a short course on that genealogy by touring the gravestones. The church in my time had about eighty members, and shared a pastor with East Brook U.P. Church. He would preach at a 9:45 a.m. service at Neshannock, and then drive to East Brook and preach the same sermon at 11:00. It was an efficient arrangement and I don't know why more small churches don't do that. (They have since separated and each has its own minister.) We would have Sunday School after church, and East Brook before. The first pastor I remember clearly was Bob Douglas, a cheerful young man fresh out of seminary who enjoyed working with young people. Dad was on the Session for decades, and was Clerk of Session for more than twenty-five years until he died.

We probably weren't much use around the farm before we got to school age, but I can remember gathering eggs in the chicken house, hoeing in the vegetable garden, and other small chores at a pretty young age. My mother, in particular, had a strong Calvinistic sense that work was good for you, and that idle hands were the devil's workshop, etc. We must have been assigned chores as soon as we could handle them, and got a modest allowance, some of which had to go to Sunday School.

I was sent off to school at age five, as my sixth birthday was before the end of the year (five seems unfashionably young now). It was first grade, there being no kindergarten, but maybe we were learning what kids get in kindergarten now. The school was Hickory Heights Elementary School, located down the hill towards New Castle, about a mile from home. We went by bus, carrying our lunch buckets, as of course there was no food service available. The first two grades were in the same room under the tutelage of Miss Copper, who seemed like an ancient and withered prune to my young eyes. She was stern and unsmiling, and brooked no nonsense from her young charges.

I doubt if I was a very good student those first two years, at least my memory is that of a struggle to keep up with the class. Maybe I was a bit young. But I passed, and when I got to third grade, I had reached the big time, because now we were housed with the fourth graders. There the teacher was Ruth Newman, a young woman who was a distant cousin of my mother. She was warm and kind, and I began to discover myself as a student. That year I did well, and developed the expectation of getting A's, or at the worst B's, and found I liked school because I was good at it. I think it is fortunate for a child to develop the illusion that he or she is good at learning, because the illusion may lead to reality. At any rate, somehow I developed this illusion about that time, and to this day I still enjoy being a student, and I remember "Miss Newman" fondly for her part in developing that sense in me.

There were about eighteen or twenty of us in a class, and we either came from farm families, most of Scotch-Irish ancestry, or were children of second-generation Italian or Polish immigrants who lived nearer New Castle. There were no blacks, no Jews, or other nationalities represented in Hickory Township, so it was far from a cosmopolitan environment. In fact, I knew no other kinds of Americans until I joined the Army, and thereafter went to college and law school.

Willard was a different case. He wasn't a bad student, but enjoyed people so much he couldn't be unduly bothered with the drudgery of studying. He was also strong-willed, and clashes with my equally strong-willed mother were frequent and noisy. When he was just learning to talk and would get mad, he would run around yelling "Poop!" which was the only swear-word he knew. At the age of seven, after a row with Mom, he packed up some of his belongings in a bandana, tied to a stick, and ran away from home. I think he got as far as Grandma's.

In contrast, I saw myself as a spectator of what was going on, at home as well as in the rest of the world, and didn't share his sense of being an active participant. My younger generation brother, Gaylord, was more like me when he got to his school years.

But we were growing up, and the farm chores increased proportionately to size, although I wonder if we weren't more of a liability than help. We learned to drive the tractor at an early age, about the time we were eleven or twelve. We had bikes to ride, and on special occasions were allowed to ride to school. When I had learned to read, I read a lot of whatever came to hand. We had subscriptions to "Boy's Life" and "The Open Road for Boys", but there weren't a lot of books available. I soon developed the reputation of being a day-dreamer, and my life-long habit of absent-mindedness developed early. I might be sent off on some errand, and would wander along thinking about something else and forget what I was supposed to be doing.

So how was the life of a boy on the farm different from that of you city kids? Well, there were the seasonal rituals of plowing, harrowing, planting, weeding and harvesting, and for each crop there was a different routine. Wheat was planted in the Fall, corn and oats in the Spring, and alfalfa and other hay fol-lowed the corn crop. The chore of hauling hay into the barn began in June or July, and was the most tedious of all. We didn't have a baler, much less the big round bales now used, so getting hay into the barn was what we would now call "labor intensive".

The hay would be cut (by tractor with mower), raked (by tractor with rake), and after drying for about two days (hoping it would not be ruined by rain), would be loaded onto a wagon, pulled by the tractor, with a hay loader trailing the wagon. One person, usually the strongest, would fork the hay from the loader onto the wagon to spread it around, with maybe another person on the front of the wagon handling that end. Driving the tractor was the easiest job, and as among Dad and Willard, I usually got that job. Eventually the wagon would be loaded and pulled into the barn. From there it had to be transported to the haymow, which was done by an elaborate arrangement with a fork inserted into the hay load, pulled up by a pulley system attached to the tractor, to the roof beam of the barn, and then run along a track to one side of the barn or the other. There it would be dropped, in a cloud of dust and hayseeds, into the mow, and moved around by hand and pitchfork to distribute it in the mow. All of this took place in hot weather, and the inside of a haymow under a slate roof in hot sun isn't the greatest working environment. But we survived it, and later in life when I found myself fretting about whatever work I was doing, I would remember that it could be worse: I could be hauling hay!

In our early years, wheat would be cut with a "binder", a machine that tied the wheat stalks into bundles weighing five pounds or so, and those bundles would be picked up by hand and built into "shocks", with about six or seven bundles in a circle, and one or two bundles on top to make a roof. Then the wheat would dry for a few days, and eventually would be threshed. This took place in early July, and threshing day was one of the big events of the year. The man who owned the big threshing machine would tow it into some field, and all the friends and neighbors that could be gathered up would come with their tractors and wagons and haul the shocks of wheat to the threshing machine, which would separate the grain from the straw, with grain going into burlap bags and the straw being blown onto a big stack in the open field. It was an exciting day; the work was strenuous and hot, and at noontime the men and boys would wash up and sit down to an enormous dinner that the women had prepared. This was the biggest meal of the whole year, usually exceeding even Thanksgiving and Christmas, if that was possible. It was also a social event, and we looked forward to the day when "the thrashers are coming".

Oats were threshed in the same way, usually in early August. Corn was either cut and ground up into ensilage to be blown into the silo, in early September, or cut, shocked and husked in October. My cousin, Bets Hackett, *nee* Elizabeth Ann Alford, reminds me of the time we had just finished filling Uncle Floyd's silo, and the whole silo collapsed, fortunately with nobody in it. What a mess! The ensilage had to be buried in the ground to preserve it for the winter.

By the time we were teenagers, in the 1940s, threshing had given way to the combine, which cut and separated the grain in one step, thus eliminating a lot of manual labor. It was more efficient, but not as much fun. Corn shocking and husking also gave way to the corn-picking machine, which picked and husked the corn mechanically. We didn't know it then, but we were living in an era of large advances in farm productivity. The result, over a period of about a hundred years, was that instead of requiring about fifty percent of the population to produce the food for everyone, only one or two percent of the people are now needed for farming. That is a large shift in employment, and for the last few decades we have been seeing a similar shift in manufacturing, with fewer people required to produce more goods. But even as boys, we could see that there wasn't much future in farming, and frankly, I didn't care for it anyway. The noted Washington lawyer, Thurman Arnold, reportedly said that he owed his great success in the practice of law to hard work: he had tried it as a boy on the farm, and opted for something else. I have often quoted him.

But I digress; this is supposed to be about what it was like growing up in the 1930s. We progressed through the first eight grades at Hickory Heights, and as we went along I grew to expect that I would get the best grades in the class. Years later, my children, students in a large school system, liked to point out that being first wasn't too difficult, as there were so few in my classes.

Whatever talent I had in the schoolroom did not manifest itself in any way in athletic efforts. When we were in 7th and 8th grades, each class had a boy's softball team. There were ten members on the team, and eleven boys in my class. People were picked for the team based on perceived ability, and the only time I got to play was when someone else was sick. I rarely got a base hit, and dreaded to have a ball hit to me in right field, where I was usually sent. One day I was almost responsible for the death or injury of the principal of the school, John Martin. A fly ball was hit to me in right field and landed on top of my head. Mr. Martin was watching this from the fire escape on the second story of the school and almost fell off laughing.

In the winters, which seemed colder than those we have had lately, we went ice skating on the ponds and in the quarries, sled riding, and skiing down the hills on the farm. Our first pair of skis was a pair of barrel staves, strapped on somehow, but we eventually got our own store-bought ones.

At some point in those years we were started on music lessons. At first, Willard and I were given piano lessons. He took to them quickly and surely, and I fumbled along. After about six or so lessons, I could see that I did not have the talent of my older brother, and asked to be excused from further struggles with the piano. I was allowed to quit, to my regret in later years.

We were then sent into New Castle to take Hawaiian guitar lessons, for what reason I can't imagine. I did passably well at this, and perhaps learned something about reading music, but the instrument was of no earthly use. Finally, when we got a little older, Willard took trumpet lessons, and I took French horn lessons. Again, his musical talent was evident, but my dogged application to the horn at least persisted, and I played that instrument through high school and in the Army band at Pennsylvania Military College, but I get ahead of the story.

Throughout our growing up, Willard displayed a clear musical talent, evidenced by his getting various instruments, such as the ukulele and the guitar, and teaching himself how to play them. I never had that sort of creativity.

But what was I like as a boy? I liked to read, and think, and dream. Most who knew me saw me as a shy, quiet, daydreamer, which seems to surprise most people who have known me only as an adult. But, to me, that still seems to be the real me, hiding underneath the protective shell in which we all encase ourselves for dealing with the world. My favorite author as a boy was Mark Twain, and I thought Tom Sawyer and Huckleberry Finn were the best books ever written. After a lifetime of reading books, I think I wasn't too far off. I also loved books about the sea, of which I knew nothing, and remember the Captain Hornblower stories particularly.

But there was a lot going on in the world outside of Lawrence County. The first presidential campaign I can remember was that of 1936: Franklin D. Roosevelt v. Alfred Landon. I certainly was raised to be a loyal Republican, as any well-bred, patriotic, real American would be, and I had an Alf Landon button with a sunflower on it. It was the first of many political disappointments for me, because he lost overwhelmingly. I remember being teased by the kids whose parents were Democrats (one headline was "Landon Gets a Goose Egg"). But I'm not prejudiced or stubborn. Despite the attempts of eggheads since then to deify FDR, I am still convinced that he was a great phony, and that Alf Landon would have been a far superior President.

But elections didn't affect our lives much, and still don't. Even the Great Depression of the 1930's made little impression, as Dad always had work and we could grow a lot of what we ate on the farm. But a lot of people were out of work, and from time to time itinerants (we called them "bums") would come to the back door of our house looking for work or for something to eat. Mom could rarely refuse to feed someone, so each would get a ham sandwich or something and go on his way. People worried about work, and sometimes one or more of my uncles would be unemployed.

Summers always arrived bringing freedom from school. Summers were different then or, more likely, they seemed different to me at that age. I remember the joy of going out in bare feet for the first time each year and the smell of new mown grass in the spring, a smell that still brings a sense of nostalgia for the past. One year on the last day of school I came down with the measles, and spent the next few days in a darkened bedroom listening to the sounds of summer outdoors and smelling that new-mown grass.

Summers were a time to visit all those cousins. Three of the families lived in Lawrence County. Aunt Florence, the oldest of my father's generation, lived in Ellwood City, with her husband, Joe Young, and their three daughters. The oldest two were several years older than Willard and me, but the youngest, Helen, was the same age as Willard. The next oldest sister, closest in age to my Dad, was Aunt Laura, who lived with her husband, Floyd Alford, on a farm about a mile and a half from us, on the County Line Road (I believe it used to have been the county line between Mercer and Beaver Counties, before Lawrence County had been created). The Alfords had four children, all about our age: Jim, Willard's age; Mary Ruth, my age; Edna Jean, two years younger, and Elizabeth Ann, about the age of Gaylord.

Aunt Margaretta was Dad's younger sister, and she lived with her family near Mr. Jackson, west of New Castle. Joe Reed was her husband, and they had four children: Dick, an older son, Bill, a year older than Willard; Eileen, my age, and Keith, a younger brother. Aunt Nancy Sewall ("Aunt Nanny" to us kids) and Uncle Carl lived in Philadelphia, as I have mentioned, with three daughters: Dorothy, about three years older than Willard, Virginia, about his age, and Florence, a year younger than me.

Uncle Tom, known to the family by his middle name, Herman, worked for the Extension Service of Penn State, first as a county agent in Erie County, then later as an administrator in State College. He and his wife, Margaret, had no children. The youngest daughter of my father's generation, Mary Elizabeth, married Wayne Vannoy, and they lived near Erie. They eventually had three boys, and the oldest died at the age of four, the first death in the family that I could recall. Mary Elizabeth, always called by both names, to distinguish her from her mother, Grandma Patton, of the same name, was only about ten years older than us kids, but was the first of her generation to die.

All of this tribe would usually appear at least once each summer for a big picnic at Grandma's, with sweet corn, fried chicken, fresh tomatoes, and all the side dishes for a big feast. The other big family holidays were Thanksgiving and Christmas, and everyone would come home to Grandma's for those days. There were so many of us that the children would be fed first, around a long table in her dining room, and the adults would eat at the second sitting. Some of the fathers would eat with us if they couldn't wait, or perhaps to maintain order.

We had the usual children's toys, including one that maybe we shouldn't have been trusted with: a BB rifle. We had great wars with neighboring kids in the quarry not far from our house, of course without the knowledge of our parents. We occasionally took pot shots at each other, and one time, Willard and I, pretending to be snipers in our upstairs bedroom window, shot Gaylord (then about five), who went crying to Mother with a bleeding thumb. We got a thorough thrashing for that episode. We regarded him as a traitor for tattling.

Life on a farm wasn't all toil and effort. I can't remember my father ever having time to play with us, in the image of the modern ideal father, but we would have an annual trip to Presque Isle in Erie each summer. With great anticipation we would start off in the morning, after the chores had been done, to drive up Route 19 to Erie, about a two hour trip. Invariably it would be a beautiful sunny summer morning, and the travel to Mercer and Meadville was exciting. When I drive up Route 79 now, I still remember the joy of those trips. As you go north from Harlansburg, the land flattens out into the glacial moraine, and provides rich farming land stretching off to the border. We would play automobile games to keep us kids amused (you get one point for each cow on your side of the car, two points for a horse, ten points for a white horse, and deduct ten points for a cemetery). It was a contest to see who could first spot the Mercer County Court House dome, and the first glimpse of that great sea, Lake Erie.

Having arrived, we would set up camp at a picnic table on Presque Isle, admire the red-headed woodpeckers and shore birds, marvel at the yachts in the marina and have our lunch (cold chicken, ham, potato salad, baked beans, lemonade and the like), and after a suitable pause we could go swimming in the lake. The pause was to honor a widely held belief that you would get a cramp and drown if you went swimming right after eating. That still doesn't make any sense to me, and I go swimming whenever I feel like it. For us boys not used to seeing such vast expanses of water, it was heaven. About mid-afternoon we would pack up and go home, as the cows had to be milked, chickens fed and reality restored. Sometimes the Alford family would join our trek, and we still have a few old photographs of all of us on one of those annual jaunts.

Once or twice I got to go to summer camp at Camp Fred Rentz on the Slippery Rock Creek, about seven or eight miles from home. (Fred Rentz was the owner of the New Castle News, and I would get to know his son Fred, Junior, many years later as a member of the Westminster College Board.) I think these were sponsored by the 4-H Club, and I would have been about eleven or twelve years old. It was a good growing up experience, sleeping in tents with other boys, away from your parents, doing the simple happy things that campers always do, swimming, volley ball, campfire singing, and all that.

There were, however, real wars going on in the world, as anyone who could read or listen to the radio was aware. A big bully named Mussolini was attacking Ethiopia, a lunatic named Adolph Hitler was raving in Berlin, and to the dismay of the missionaries of the United Presbyterian Church, Japan was having its way with China. The Civil War in Spain was a preview of coming events in Europe, with fascists squaring off against communists. It wasn't clear that the United States would be involved, but memories of the Great War, soon to become merely World War I, were fresh in adult minds and the tensions between "isolationists" and "internationalists" were publicly debated, a debate that events would soon render moot.

3

The War Years

If you have been studying your history books, you know that Germany, with the connivance of the Soviet Union, attacked Poland in September, 1939, setting off the great war of my time, soon designated World War II. But you would not have learned from your history books, until this one, that I was then entering the seventh grade at Hickory Heights.

After the bullies polished off the Polish, nothing much happened the following winter. France was hunkered down behind its Maginot Line with its Grand Armee. I don't recall anything noteworthy happening in my life, either. Years go by in which your life is changing and you don't notice the change until something striking occurs. School begins to get a little more interesting about this time, but I wrack my brain to remember why.

The spring brought instant action, of the most devastating sort to the Allies. The German Army ignored the Maginot Line, overran Belgium and knocked the great army of France out in one quick punch. The British barely managed to pull most of their army out at Dunkirk with the help of a lot of little boats. So now the madman, Hitler, had reached his pinnacle, but he didn't know it.

And what has this to do with ordinary peoples lives, like mine? In the short run, not much. We went on growing up as usual. By then we were members of the 4-H Club, the motto of which was "learning by doing", a motto I have followed all my life, especially in my professional life, where I discovered people would pay you while you were learning. (They don't call it the practice of law without reason) So what was it we did? Well, at first we raised capons. If you raise a bunch of baby chicks, a certain number of them, let's say half, will turn out to be roosters, which don't serve any socially useful function like laying eggs. Young men, keep that in mind. So what are roosters good for, apart from the one in a hundred needed to perpetuate the species? Try fried chicken, for one, and you are onto a good thing. To enhance this value, turn them into capons and they will command a premium price (maybe worth slightly more than the feed you poured into them). They are worth more as roasting chickens, because they have more white meat and therefore taste better if you happen to like white meat, as any sensible person does. I still like capon better than any other fowl.

So how do you turn these worthless little roosters into capons? About the time the chicks are starting to shed their down and replace that with feathers, the County Agent would come out to our 4-H group, and would show us how to make a neat incision between the ribs and surgically remove their little testicles, about the size of a grain of rice. Actually, he would do the operation on most of the chicks, and we would get to practice on one or two of them. I preferred to watch him do it, thereby indicating I didn't have an innate compulsion to be a surgeon. Without any anesthetic or post-op procedures, most survived and would be fine in a few days. If the surgeries were successful, the capons would develop more weight than they would as roosters, and by Thanksgiving or Christmas at the latest would be a nice eight pounds or more of prime roasting material. If the operation wasn't completely successful, you would have a "slip", which was somewhere between a rooster and a capon. He, or it, would develop a red comb, maybe even try to crow, ineffectually, and strut around like a rooster, but among the cognoscenti he wouldn't cut it. So maybe some of them could be passed off as capons in the fall, and if not, we would eat them.

Well, given the economic advantages we had, it was a sure-fire money maker. First of all, our parents would buy the chicks. Then they would pay for the feed, housing, and provide the space for them without charge. Now we would call them "free range capons" because they would live in a coop out in the field and were free to go out every day and wander around and scratch in the dirt. It is quite likely that the chicken sandwich you just ate wasn't raised like that, as most chickens are now raised in cages, and never see the sky or the ground, but why get sentimental about that, as chickens are among the dumbest creatures you are likely to meet. What we had to do was make sure they had water, chicken feed (and I don't mean small change) and didn't get eaten up by foxes, weasels, wild dogs and the like, which mostly meant we were supposed to close the chicken coop doors in the evening and open them in the morning.

So we became small-time entrepreneurs, without much attention to the cost/revenue equation, which if we had been able to figure out would probably have discouraged us. Before I leave the subject of chickens, though, I have to tell you about a dog we had about that time, named "Guy", who was a Scottish Border Collie, a remarkably intelligent breed bred to herd sheep. Well we didn't have any sheep, so he would try to herd anything, cows, pigs or people, it was just built into his genes. The limits of his intelligence were shown when he tried to herd chickens, which after he got them into a reasonably small group would suddenly fly off in all directions leaving him in a state of total frustration. It was worth the price of admission just to see the look of disgust in his face. We should have sent him to a dog psychoanalyst.

The depression was still in full swing in the late 30s (FDR never did find a solution for that, because he was on the wrong track), and one of my younger uncles, Wayne Vannoy, who I think was out of work, came to stay at Grandma's. He got the great idea one Spring to make maple syrup from the sap of the maple trees back in the pasture at the rear, or north end, of the farm. In concept, it's not a difficult job: you drill a hole in a maple tree, stick a wooden tube into it, put a bucket under the spout, and wait for it to fill up with sap. Then all you have to do is boil the sap to evaporate the water, and *voila* you get maple syrup, and if you keep on boiling it you get maple sugar. If you have a lot of patience you too can make maple syrup. Well, it's a job that appeals to the boyscout in all of us, and Wayne, bless his heart, was still at about that level, and quickly enlisted Willard and me in his endeavor. With a number of maple trees you get a lot of gallons of sap, and it wasn't worth hauling all that back to the house, so the initial boiling-evaporation was done in a big iron kettle on an open fire in the woods. Having been a good scout, he taught us to burn off the dead grass around the fireplace before leaving it for the night. So one evening we three were burning off the grass around the fire, when a wind came up and started to spread the fire throughout the woods which were quite dry. We kept stamping and trying to put the fire out (no water being readily available), but it kept getting ahead of us. Being the most dispensable member of this crew, I was dispatched to race back home and bring help. Being more that a little terrified about what damage we were about to create, imagining a conflagration that would destroy the world as we knew it, I raced as fast as my little legs would carry me to report this disaster. I found Dad and breathlessly reported our misfeasance, which he accepted with remarkable aplomb. He gathered up several burlap sacks, dunked them in water, and we hurried back to the scene. Well, we hadn't burned down the woods, but the brave fire fighters were glad to see the cavalry arrive, and we soon beat out the blaze.

As you might gather, we raised a lot of the food we ate on the farm. A big vegetable garden in the Summer would produce plenty to keep my mother canning for weeks, giving us beans, peas, tomatoes and the like for the whole winter. We tried raising potatoes a few times, but that wasn't worth all the effort. We had apple trees and cherry and pear trees, and the cherries could be canned and the apples kept in cold storage over the winter. Peaches, usually grown by somebody else, would also be canned. Carrots would keep in their raw state for several months, and were also canned. When I say "canned", I mean sealed in glass "*Atlas*" jars of quart size or smaller. My mother also used to dry sweet corn on a dryer in the basement. It was great all winter, and I still enjoy the flavor of dried corn sauteed in milk.

Much of the meat we ate was also raised at home. Dad would butcher one or two hogs each fall or winter, cure them in cool weather, and we would have pork roasts, sausage, ham, bacon and all those other great sources of fat that we now know are so bad for us. There were always plenty of fresh eggs, and we had them for breakfast every morning, and on my low cholesterol diet now I sometimes curse the scientists who figured out that a breakfast of eggs, sausage and fried potatoes isn't the best thing in the world for you. Occasionally he would butcher a cow or young steer, and we would have hamburg, roasts and steak, or more likely, he would buy a quarter of beef from another farmer, and do the same with it. You can get pretty tired of beef when you try to eat up a whole cow before it spoils. At that time, refrigeration was still in its infancy, and the development of freezers was one of the great new ideas of my youth. When these were first developed, we could rent a locker in a freezer in New Castle, sort of like a safe deposit box, as nobody had heard of having a freezer in your own home.

One of the differences I have noticed over the years is that this kind of youth left one with fairly realistic and unsentimental views about animals. You raised them, killed them and ate them. Most of the human carnivores raised in the city think that meat comes nicely wrapped from butcher shops, and don't give much thought to how it got there. Maybe it's better for the appetite to preserve that illusion.

So while life went on, so did the war. There was some fear that began to spread even to boys, and I remember a nightmare of waves of bombers flying over our house carrying an irresistible force attacking us. This probably came from seeing newsreels at the movies showing the conquest of France and the air battle over Britain. Hitler seemed to be unstoppable.

So I moved on to eighth grade in September 1940, and Willard was now grown up, because in the ninth grade you went to High School at East Brook, and the kids graduating from our elementary school were merged with the kids from the East Brook elementary school to become the freshman class in high school. That was about three miles away, but they traveled in the same bus as we young fry. For historical purposes, I should add that none of these schools exist today, and haven't for decades, as they have all been merged into a bigger school district called "Laurel", which includes several townships in eastern Lawrence County.

In the eighth grade, we were now the big kids in that small pond, and our teacher was John Martin, a lantern-jawed, no-nonsense disciplinarian, whose chief claim to distinction was that he had spent a year living in Juneau, Alaska, a feat that prompted interminable reminiscences. We didn't like him, but we were sufficiently cowed to refrain from most overt trouble. He wielded an impressive paddle on the boys, and he could intimidate the girls with a terrifying stare. I think he wasn't a bad teacher, if rather uninspiring; his style was to sort of grind the subject matter into us.

I was a fairly small boy, and didn't grow real fast until the next year, when I shot up several inches to normal size, although still a bit skinny.

Willard and one of our neighbors, Joe Sickafuse, came up with a bright idea for making an impression in high school. Joe was a fun-loving boy in the grade ahead of Willard, and they decided to make a tandem bike and ride it to school. They didn't have a tandem bike, but they took the front wheel off of Joe's and attached the fork to the rear axle of Willard's. If you think about it, there is something structurally unsound about this, as the resulting bike doesn't have a cross bar the length of the bike for stability. So it was kind of wobbly but they found they could ride it and set off to school, going the short route of about three miles along the back roads. One of these roads was a dirt road, with a steep hill and a sharp curve, and was called the "*Devil's Elbow*" road. About the time they got to the elbow, the bike collapsed and sent them sprawling over the road. After wiping themselves off, they walked to school and got somebody to haul the remains back later.

Well, finally in the fall of 1941, I was off to East Brook High School, having arrived at that stage called "puberty", but we won't discuss how I discovered that. I was thirteen, going on fourteen. Whatever happened in my life that term pales into insignificance by the events in the world. On a quiet Sunday afternoon, two days before my birthday, we came in from the barn after the evening chores to hear the electrifying news: the Japanese had bombed Pearl Harbor and wiped out most of our Pacific fleet. The hubris leading to that surprise attack, the worst mistake the Japanese could have made, still puzzles me. They gained a short-lived tactical advantage, but had awakened the sleeping giant of the United States to a fury that was breathtaking. Just about every man, woman and child was ready to pick up a gun and start shooting.

None of us who lived through the next four years would ever see the country so united in one purpose: defeat the Axis powers. There was nothing to debate except ways and means, and that was usually left to the military and the top political leaders of the country. It was, of course, the realization of the fondest hopes of Winston Churchill, who despite his brave words knew that Britain alone didn't have a chance against Germany.

But Hitler had made a similar fatal error. Having failed to bomb Britain into submission, he decided that game wasn't worth the effort, and turned on his erstwhile ally, the Soviet Union. He should have read the history of Napoleon, and probably had, but had been unimpressed. So now he found himself fighting the British in North Africa, the Russians on their home territory, and after December 7, the United States wherever it chose, which at first, was North Africa.

On the home front, everything changed now that the war was real. The boys who had graduated from high school the previous year, along with some who had not, were joining the Army, Navy or Marines (the Air Force came later), or were being drafted. This country started rationing food and gasoline, even though the rationing of either was entirely unnecessary, but it made people feel like they were at war and were participating in some way.

As you can imagine from my description of where our food came from, food rationing didn't have much effect on us: we grew it ourselves. But I do remember that we had to be careful about sugar, which restraint was no doubt very healthful. Gas rationing was a different story, or at least seemed to be when we got to be sixteen and got drivers' licenses. Dad had a "B" card for gasoline rationing, which meant he could get all the gas he needed for work, although there was some limit as to what that was. However, gasoline for tractors was unrationed, so there was always a tank full of gasoline available for that, and what could stop you from filling up with that. But it gave my parents a good excuse if they didn't want us running around in the car.

My mother had her own car when we were young, a black 1930 Buick sedan, which I would love to own now. But she sold this, maybe because of the war, and then we had whatever Dad was driving, usually a Plymouth or Ford sedan. Learning to drive wasn't a very big deal for kids who had been driving a tractor for years, but you did have to learn how to use a clutch with the foot, as the John Deere had a hand clutch. Of course, there wasn't anything like an automatic transmission available then.

In school, we had the usual array of secondary education courses. I took two years of Latin, and was later grateful for that as a base for the Romance languages (Spanish was my language in college), and as a help in learning a few phrases in whatever country in Europe in which we might travel. It may have been some help with legal Latin in law school. I got as far as second year Algebra and plane and solid geometry, and thought I was fairly good at math (I would discover my limits later).

History was not nearly as fascinating as the all-consuming history that was happening all about us. I greatly enjoyed the literature courses, and did well at writing. I particularly remember one very good teacher, America Robinson, who was our next—door neighbor. She was a quiet but inspiring teacher of the classic texts, and I associate much of my life-long enjoyment of reading with her example. Teachers do make a great difference in our lives, and I am grateful for all those who have changed mine.

One small anecdote about Mrs. Robinson: in my junior year, a girl in our class was having difficulty writing some paper for English class. She happened to be dating Willard at the time, and asked me to help her write one. I cheerfully dashed off something, and when she turned it in, Mrs. Robinson had her stand up in class and read this splendid example. I think she was suspicious of the origin of the work, as the nominal author hadn't shown great promise previously. However, both parties to the academic fraud kept mum, and while I may have been suspected, I wasn't accused. I got the message, however: don't try that again.

I liked to sing then, as I still do, and I sang in the high school choir, and in a quartet that consisted of Willard as first tenor, me as lead, Elmer Morrow as baritone, and Ralph Robinson, bass. We sang a variety of music: barbershop, male quartet, religious, whatever came along. We were invited to sing at a few places beside school, mostly churches, and we weren't bad. One of our tricks when singing before a strange audience was to ask them to pick out the two of us who were brothers. People would invariably pick some combination of Ralph, Elmer and I, and would be surprised to find out that Willard and I were the brothers, as we didn't look at all alike.

I still prefer quartet singing over all other forms of singing. There is nobody else to carry your part, and you have to listen to the others to produce a balanced blend. It is a pleasing combination of individual and group effort. Duet singing isn't bad, but a lot of that is just alternate solos. I have always been a tenor, which is fortunate, as there are never enough of them to go around, so I have never had any problem finding non-paying singing jobs.

There was some social life in high school, even in wartime. We had occasional parties, not a lot that I remember, and I went out on dates with girls in my class. I never found any special girl friend, or maybe it was *vice versa*, none seemed smitten with me.

In the winter of my junior year, one of us (I don't remember who) had a brilliant idea for enhancing our social status. Ralph Robinson lived on a farm behind us, and they had an old horse. There was an old sleigh sitting in the rafters of Grandma's barn, and it hadn't been used in decades. Why didn't we hitch the horse to the sleigh and ride to school some snowy morning? We could take girls for sleigh rides and be a big hit. On a Sunday afternoon when we had about a foot of snow on the ground, Ralph brought the horse over and we hitched him to the sleigh. With sleigh bells jingling, we rode around the fields that afternoon in practice for the great event. Conditions were perfect. The anticipation of our coup was overwhelming.

Ralph was back in the morning with horse, and Willard and I joined him for the triumphant ride to school. We went back through our woods, headed for the Robinsons, on the way to school. The poor old horse, no doubt stiff and sore from the previous day's exercise, was headed for his barn and couldn't wait to get there. He went faster and faster, down the hill to the bottom of a ravine where the ancient sleigh hit a ditch at high speed and completely disintegrated. The horse just kept running until he got to his barn, leaving us sitting in the snow with only the brittle remnants of that dried out old sleigh around us. You may remember a poem about the "Wonderful One Horse Shay" that was so well built that no part ever wore out until the shay disintegrated all at once? That was us. We didn't think it was funny then, but I would pay well for a videotape of that scene now. That was the end of a great idea.

So what was I doing to help the war effort? Willard and I joined the American Legion band in New Castle. That got us uniforms and practice at close-order drill. He played the trumpet, and I the horn. I thought we were pretty good, as marching bands go, but I didn't have much basis for comparison. Well, about once a month or so, we would go to the Pennsylvania Railroad station in New Castle of a Saturday morning and serenade the latest group of draftees or enlistees going off to serve their country. I enjoyed it, and kept on doing it my senior year, after having serenaded Willard as he went off to join the Navy the Summer of 1944. We played for the usual parades around New Castle, and I remember going to Beaver Falls to play on one cold Thanksgiving morning. The French horn has a small mouthpiece, and I took it off the horn and kept it in my mouth when we weren't playing, to keep from freezing my lip.

It was quite fashionable then to have a vegetable garden, given rationing and the wartime propaganda. They were called "Victory Gardens", and if we could grow enough vegetables we would beat the Huns and the Japs. Since we were already growing all we could eat, this didn't seem like much of a contribution. Industry was booming, of course, and everybody had a job, but to be a hero, you had to be in uniform. Wartime movies were great, and probably produced more enlistments than any other kind of propaganda. We bought "E" bonds with our savings, and they had books of stamps that kids could buy, and when you filled one up, you got an $18.75 bond that would be worth $25 when it matured in ten years. That was my first experience in investing in U.S. Treasuries.

We had a basketball team at East Brook, and we played in a league with eight other country schools. We were usually in serious contention for last place, with a little school at Wampum the perennial first place team. They had a coach named Butler Hennon who started kids shooting basketballs about the time they were in first grade, and by the time they got to high school, all were deadly one-handed shooters. I wasn't enough of an athlete to make our team, so I enlisted as team manager. I got to look after the uniforms, help the coach, and act as scorer or timekeeper at the games. I traveled with the team to away games, so I saw the schools attended by my cousins: Shenango for the Alfords, and Mt. Jackson for the Reeds.

At the Mt. Jackson games, I met a fellow named Glenn Reed, who would later become my college and law school roommate, and friend for life, which, alas, in his case, wasn't too long. Anyway, he was the manager of his basketball team, and our two teams were close rivals. The home team manager was the official time-keeper, so I found myself in that usually quiet position at our last home game, both Glenn and I being seniors. The game was close, and as it wound down, we had a one-point lead. As the game ending buzzer sounded, Mt. Jackson had the ball, and their center made a desperate throw from mid-court which miraculously went through the hoop. If it counted, they won, and if not, we did. The referees were undecided, so they came to me as official timekeeper for the decision. "*Time expired before he released the ball*" was my prompt decision, which produced impassioned tirades from Glenn and his whole team. To no avail, of course; there wasn't any instant replay. But I have often replayed that scene in my mind, and to this day I still don't know whether the ball was out of his hands when I pushed the buzzer or not. It was close, so clearly I made the right decision. It was the only basketball game I ever won.

By the time I got to be a senior, in 1944, the Allies had opened the second front in Europe, and we were rolling up the Pacific isles, one by one. Casualties were heavy, and gold stars began to appear in the windows of our neighbors. One of those, Joe Sickafuse, the fun-loving creator of the tandem bike, was killed in Italy, and my cousins, Dick and Bill Reed were in combat in Italy and France. Willard had gone into the Navy, and was assigned to a minesweeper in the North Atlantic, and later to a PC boat. One of his classmates was killed in a kamikaze attack in the Pacific. We were enjoying our last year at East Brook, and wondering what the next year would bring. It looked as though I might get into the Service in time for the attack on Japan.

I sometimes reflect on the exuberance of youth that made us all want to get into the military and go off to war. I now think that those of us born in 1927 were rather lucky to have avoided wartime service, but at the time we felt most unlucky to be missing the great adventure of our lives. Forty years later I met a German who was about two years younger than I. Herr Kalvilage was an assistant plant manager for Armstrong in Muenster. We had a long talk at lunch one day, and he told me how disappointed he was, in 1945, that he was too young to fight in the German Army. As a member of the Hitler Youth, he would have been happy to enlist, but he had promised his father, shortly before he left for the Russian front (never to be seen again), that he would not volunteer. They were accepting 14-year old boys at the end, and many of his classmates enlisted and disappeared forever. He was a nice person, intelligent and personable, and we both left that lunch grateful that our patriotic childhood ambition to kill each other had not been gratified.

So the war wound down about the same time as my high school education was ending. I got the opportunity to enlist in the Army Specialized Training Reserve Program in April 1945. The arrangement was that the Army would send you to college for a semester or two until you became 18, and then off you went to the Regular Army. Since my 18th birthday wasn't until December, it meant that I could get in two semesters, which seemed like a happy arrangement. One had to have good grades, pass a test and take a physical, and I qualified. The war in Europe ended in May, but we were anticipating another year or so before the assault on Japan.

President Roosevelt died that spring, leaving his Vice President, Harry Truman in charge of the war. At the end of May 1945, I graduated from East Brook. I suppose it was like most graduations, but there were only two dozen of us, so it didn't take long. I was the valedictorian, and got to make some remarks, but happily I have forgotten what profound insights I laid on the suffering audience. We had caps and gowns, and I suppose somebody played "Pomp and Circumstances" on a piano so that we could process.

The excitement over the end of the war in Europe had hardly subsided, when a new sensation was announced. We had bombed Hiroshima with a new weapon called the "*Atomic Bomb*", and Harry Truman called for the Japanese to surrender. They procrastinated, and we dropped a second one on Nagasaki. Only the

Japanese could see the horror of this weapon, and they then promptly surrendered. I have never regretted this decision by the United States, for while it killed thousands of innocent people, it stopped the war and kept even more thousands from being killed on both sides.

Willard was then steaming across the Pacific, having called at Pearl Harbor, where the Navy was being assembled for the attack on Japan. They turned around and came home. His view was that the Japanese had never apologized for Pearl Harbor, and we didn't need to apologize for the atomic bomb. Doubts about the use of the bomb only came later, and mostly from people who were in no danger from the war.

4

You're In the Army!

Well, the great day finally arrived. In early September 1945, my orders were to report to Pennsylvania Military College in Chester, Pennsylvania. If you are looking for that school now, desist, because after the war it became Widener College. But at that time it was a military prep school that was existing largely on the ASTRP program. What excitement! There was no doubt in my mind that this was a major passage in my life, as I took the Pennsylvania Railroad overnight to Philadelphia and down to Chester. Here I am, age seventeen going on eighteen, headed both for college and the Army. Away from home, parents, family and farm for the first time in my life.

I didn't sleep a wink that night on the train (of course, the Army didn't pay for a Pullman berth). We arrived at PMC in the morning, bleary-eyed but ready for whatever the Army had in mind for us, which was to issue uniforms, bedding, and assign us to quarters. In my case, that was Dyer Hall, an old Victorian house in Chester, just in front of the College Main Building. I was in a small room with four roommates, bunk beds and small desks for each. I am sorry to say that I can't remember their names, but they were decent boys, one from Tennessee, the others from Pennsylvania and New Jersey. I remember finally collapsing on my bunk for a nap by early afternoon.

The next day, we began to learn something about being in the Army. There were several days for orientation, learning how to report for Reveille and Tattoo, learning close-order drill, being assigned to squads, platoons, companies, and ultimately, the Battalion. We were mixed in with second semester ASTRP students who formed the student officer and non-com corps. I didn't know it at the time, but the Battalion Commander that first semester was Gregg Kerr, whom I would meet a few years later as one of my associates in the law firm I joined (but let's not get ahead of our story). There were also a few regular army officers and non-coms to provide discipline, know-how and color to the whole business.

And then we got down to the business intended, which was attending classes. It was a first year engineering curriculum, with emphasis on math, physics, English and about what you would expect in a freshman first semester. It was called an "*accelerated schedule*", which simply meant that we were expected to complete the first semester in three months. Now that I think about it, that is about the right pace for a no-nonsense curriculum. We had to study hard, but since we were also subject to army discipline, that wasn't too difficult. Your free time was spent in studying, not in social activities, as in most colleges.

If you behaved yourself, defined as not getting more that nine demerits each week, you were allowed to leave on Saturday afternoon, and not have to be back until Taps on Sunday evening. This was great for me, because I had the Sewalls to visit in Philadelphia each weekend. They couldn't have been nicer to me, providing me with a place to live, the company of my three cousins, their friends, a church on Sunday morning in which I was welcome to sing in the choir, and a chance to get to know the great city of Philadelphia. In addition, I was in uniform, and could mix with all the army people coming home from the war, and share in the general excitement of the times caused by the returning heroes. It was only a half hour trip by train from Chester to the 30th Street Station, and during that fall and winter I got to know and love that great city.

I don't recall getting into much difficulty with the discipline, but a few incidents come to mind. Being now a grown-up, I thought I should smoke, and tried cigarettes. We were not allowed to smoke in front of the Main Building, but one day I wandered up the circular drive leading to it with some friends, smoking a cigarette, where I met the Colonel and some officers. I had the cigarette in my right hand and tried saluting with my left. It wasn't a very convincing effort, and I got enough demerits to keep me in my room that weekend.

I did okay that first semester, ending in November. We had analytic and solid geometry, trigonometry, physics (in which I did poorly), English, history and other easier freshman college courses. I assumed that with all the math the Army was preparing me for the Field Artillery, which is where Dad had served in World War I. I came to learn that the Army does not follow that simple sort of logical thinking, as I eventually ended up in the Medical Corps. However, that was several months ahead, the war had ended, and who could see that far.

I still played the French horn, and was soon in the post's band. We played for parades and reviews, and it was enjoyable. I got to go home on Thanksgiving (I hitchhiked across the Pennsylvania Turnpike) and don't remember ever being homesick. We didn't get any pay while in the Reserves, but there was little need for money. Our food and uniforms were provided, and one didn't have much opportunity to spend money. My mother later gave me a packet of letters I had written her during this time, and I find it surprising that my attitudes, sense of humor, and reaction to the events of my world at that time weren't that much different than now. Do the experiences of adult life change us very much?

I didn't mind the military life. It was all new and different and boys of that age are easily amenable to its discipline. Had I been a few years older, I think I would have found it stifling. The military services know what they are doing in recruiting eighteen year olds.

In the second semester, beginning in December, the work got a little more difficult. We had calculus, and for the first time I could see that a few of my companions were coping with that subject better than I did. I worked my way through it, but it was more by rote than through understanding. It's a humbling experience to find that you have limits in any area, and this was the first for me in the academic field. I had considered what I should study when I got into a real college, and engineering had been one possibility, but this experience caused me to conclude that maybe my talents lay elsewhere.

I greatly enjoyed my weekends in Philadelphia with the Sewalls, and I still feel that Philadelphia, like Boston, is a second home to me. My Aunt Nanny and Uncle Carl could not have been kinder, and my cousins would generously include me in their lives. I went bowling with Uncle Carl, sang in the church choir with Dorothy and Virginia, went to parties and had such a great time I never had any reason to be homesick.

After one weekend in February I came back to Chester with a very sore throat. In the morning, I had a fever, but turned out for Reveille. While standing at attention, I passed out, was gathered up and taken to the infirmary. The diagnosis was a strep throat, and I was given the new miracle drug, penicillin. They didn't have it in the form of nice little pills, so I got a shot of it in my rear every three hours. By the time I recovered, my rear was in worse shape than my throat. It wasn't the best time to be in bed, as final exams were coming up soon, but I managed to get out of bed in time for them, and I struggled through the tests. I did manage to get a "B" in calculus, but I don't know why. That ended my career at PMC, as I was now eighteen, and I had a week or so of leave before reporting to Fort Meade, Maryland. I felt rather weak after the strep throat, and was glad to have the time to rest at home.

5

The Regular Army

The few days at home went quickly, and I reported to Ft. George G. Meade, Maryland (you Civil War buffs may remember that incompetent general from the battle of Gettysburg). It was known as a "*repple depple*", argot for a replacement depot. People were sent there for a short stay while the Army decided what to do with them. If one were to design a place likely to produce homesickness, boredom and a desire to escape, it would look like a repple depple. Thousands of soldiers awaiting assignment, killing time, shooting craps, stealing anything not nailed down, and hoping for a cushy assignment. Everybody is a stranger, and no use in making friends, because you are all going off in different directions. Happily it doesn't last long, and in a few days I got my orders: I was assigned to the Medical Corps (goodbye Artillery dreams) and assigned to Ft. Sam Houston in San Antonio for basic training.

I did have one decision to make before being sworn in: did I want to serve in the Reserves for "the duration", which meant for about a year, or as soon as the Army chose to get rid of its draftees, or did I want to enlist in the Regular Army for eighteen months. It was March of 1946, and I saw no advantage in getting out of the Army the following spring, as I wouldn't be able to go to college until September. The eighteen month enlistment would get me out in time for college the next Fall and I would have the additional months of the G.I. Bill to help pay for my education. The G.I. Bill was an enlightened benefit of military service: for every month of service one got a month of college education paid for by the taxpayers. It turned out to be a fortunate choice because by the time I got into Law School we were into the Korean War, and people who had less than a year of service were being drafted. As an eighteen-month veteran, I could wave goodbye to those departing.

Several hundred of us were packed into a troop train and shipped off like slow freight for Texas. A troop train isn't much of an improvement over the repple depple, but at least you are going somewhere, and after about three days we arrived in sunny San Antonio. Ft. Sam is the home of a large Army hospital, and it had a basic training camp, housing several companies of new recruits with the object of converting them into soldiers in eight weeks.

So now I was in the Third Platoon of Baker Company, and we got our first look at our sergeant, and vice versa, and one look at this undisciplined, smelly and generally disheveled group of would-be soldiers produced a well practiced tirade of what he was going to do to us in the next few weeks, none of which would bear repeating in polite company.

Most of us were eighteen years old, but there were a few old geezers in their twenties thrown in. The sergeant and our first lieutenant were old combat veterans who had decided to stay in the Army after the war, and were probably in their mid-twenties.

Life in basic training is supposed to be hell on earth for the recruits, but for eighteen-year old boys it is also a bit of a lark. Hiking, camping, calisthenics, shooting rifles and no more mental activity than could be handled by a retarded mind. After a week or so, the keen-eyed cadre could see that I knew the manual of arms (the benefit of a military prep school) could march and seemed generally cheerful, so I was made a squad leader. In basic, this doesn't lead to any stripes on the arm; after all, one was just playing at being squad leader. But it had one large advantage: the four squad leaders got a separate room at the end of the barracks, and didn't have to sleep in the open squad room with all the rest of the snorers.

We also got to lead the squad (about twelve "men") in close order drill practice, and occasionally the whole platoon when the sergeant felt like standing in the shade. I can close my eyes and still enjoy the memory of counting cadence, deciding whether to "squad right" or just the opposite, and slapping an M-1 rifle into "present arms". There is something mindlessly beguiling about military life.

Being with the same small group night and day for eight weeks, you make a few friends, maybe a few enemies, and develop some sense of group pride. I followed the advice of my father and my Uncle Carl, also a W.W.I veteran, and tried to stay out of trouble. But one day, I got into a small scrape that tested my friendships. We were given a barrel of mixed nuts, in their shells, at the mess hall at lunch time, and I filled up my fatigue pockets with them and brought them back to the barracks. Having no place to store them, I squirreled them away under the pillow on my cot, and reported for the afternoon activities.

At the end of the day, during the usual rest period before chow, our platoon was told to stay for further drill. We were marched around, double-timed and made to feel as miserable and tired as the miserable and tired sergeant could do. Finally, at the end of the hour, he announced that this punishment was because the Captain, during an inspection of the barracks, had found *nuts* in the bed of one of the squad leaders. He grimly did not identify the culprit, leaving to me to confess to the platoon my guilt, which I promptly did. There were some dark mutterings about a "G.I.shower", but I had enough friends that nothing came of that. I since have thought how happy the inspecting officer must have been, as it provided a great opportunity to teach once more the Army code: if one guy screws up, everybody suffers.

I did get into an altercation with one of the guys, and in the private dispute resolution mode of the Army, we were invited to settle the argument with boxing gloves after evening chow. I wasn't terribly enthusiastic about this, as the other guy was a lot tougher. He also was a lot better boxer, so after getting knocked down, nose bloodied, and eye blackened, I conceded the correctness of his philosophic point, whatever it was. We went out and had a beer and became friends for life, but of course I never saw him again after basic training was over.

The last week of basic was spent on bivouac, which meant we got to hike out into the jungle around San Antone, with our rifles and all our gear, sleep in our pup tents, and enjoy war maneuvers. Sleeping on the ground with only a blanket isn't great fun, but when you get tired enough, it's just fine. We had to shake out our boots in the morning to make sure there weren't any tarantulas in them, and we spent some time each day spearing rattlesnakes with bayonets, but we knew when the week ended we would be through with basic. So the last night came, and since it was a warm and cloudless evening, we all packed up our tents and gear to be ready for an early start to march back to the base. However, in the middle of the night, we were caught by a sudden thunderstorm that dropped about an inch of rain on our bare heads. There were no lights, and we didn't have flashlights, so the whole company was marched back to camp like a bunch of bedraggled rats. The gear was left strewn in the field, and eventually hauled back to camp in the morning. We were sent to sort out our underwear, socks, etc., which, considering it all looked alike, was a bit difficult. What a mess.

Hell hath no fury like a basic training cadre whose charges have made them look bad and on whom they can no longer take out their spite. If they could have, they would have made us take basic training all over again, but the new recruits were arriving, and all they could do was give us a tongue lashing and send us off to be good soldiers wherever we were going. In my case, that was deeper into the heart of Texas.

6

El Paso del Norte

The orders were to report to William Beaumont General Hospital, located in El Paso, Texas, and the Army will arrange the transportation, thank you. Along with several others from my company, I reported to the Annex at Beaumont, a group of barracks located down on the plain below the hospital. We spent a few weeks there while the Corps tried to figure out what to do with us. The Army had understood I could type, so I was classified as a clerk-typist, and soon sent to work in a medical supply room at the hospital.

The hospital is located on the east slope of the mountains, part of the Rockies, leading north from El Paso. The pass for which the city is named is cut by the Rio Grande as it runs south from New Mexico and turns east to make the Texas-Mexico border. The post was good looking, with palm trees and lawns of green grass overlooking the vast arid plain of West Texas and the large neighboring posts of Ft. Bliss and an Air Force base. It was summer 1946, and hot as hell on the desert, but pleasantly air conditioned at the hospital.

The job in the medical supply room lasted a few weeks, and about the only thing I learned was that medical alcohol mixed with grapefruit juice was an acceptable potation. I was soon transferred to work in the post Adjutant's office, which was headed by a WAC Captain, who was rumored to be the girlfriend of the Commanding Officer. I can't confirm the rumor, but he did come to call on her frequently, particularly at the end of the day. She was as homely as a horse, but was cheerful and pleasant to talk to. She soon found out that I could not only type, but could actually write letters, which seemed to be beyond her capacity, so I soon found myself doing most of her correspondence. That kind of talent gets one quickly promoted, and I became a Corporal, which was worth at least five bucks more a month. I had found a mentor in the Army.

The work of the Hospital was to provide medical services for the wounded still returning from overseas, largely the Pacific, and for the large Army bases located nearby. It wasn't a bad place in which to spend my Army career, and I soon learned to like the desert and the area. El Paso was then about ninety percent Hispanic, and you only had to cross the river to be in Mexico. We lived in air-conditioned barracks, but I had no special privileges, and had to sleep in the squad room.

Working in the Adjutant's office was a simple nine-to-five job. That left the evenings and weekends (after noon on Saturday) free to explore El Paso, Juarez (just across the Rio Grande) and surrounding countryside. I liked El Paso, particularly after the heat of the summer had passed. The high (about 4,000 feet above sea level), dry climate is great in fall and spring, and fairly mild in winter. The air was clear, there wasn't much industry then, and it would have been ideal for stargazing if I had known any astronomy then, which I didn't.

When we went across the border, we usually went in groups, as Juarez was a rough and tough border town, and it was better not to be wandering around alone. I hadn't had much experience in drinking alcohol, other than beer, and on an early trip to Juarez I learned a lesson I haven't forgotten. We were wandering around the bars of the town, where most drinks cost about fifteen cents, and we started ordering whatever pretty green, blue, purple or rainbow colored drink they seemed to be serving. That was a sure recipe for getting sick, which I promptly did on returning to camp. That wasn't the last lesson I had to learn about drinking, but it was the beginning of learning a little discretion.

We had movies on the base, usually about four or five a week. Admission was only fifteen cents, but after a few months, I found I could get an evening job at the post theatre, which got me into all the movies free, and filled up the idle time. My first job was as ticket-taker, but I finally moved up to cashier, which paid better. I don't remember what we got paid, but it probably wasn't much more than a dollar or so an hour, but then there were all those free movies. I was also trying to save money for college, and the extra income helped.

I was thinking about what I wanted to do after the Army, and one day pondering this subject, sitting on an Army bus going down to the Annex, I came to the conclusion that I wanted to be a lawyer. I had thought about this while in high school, but I didn't know any lawyers and didn't know much about what they did, other than what I had gathered from reading a few books. It seems like a strange decision looking back on it; I didn't really know what I was deciding, but I thought it was about time I made up my mind, so I did. Happily, I never questioned that decision and proceeded to carry out that conclusion from then on.

The Army decided about that time that it would determine enlisted rank promotions based on a written test of some sort. I took one, and was promoted to sergeant, just about the time of my nineteenth birthday. I liked the three stripes on my sleeve, and the extra pay of a few dollars a month. A few months later they repeated the test, and I became a staff sergeant. Those were the easiest promotions I ever received.

In the Spring of 1947, I signed up for a trip to escort a patient to a veterans hospital in Canandaigua, New York. These junkets were one of the perks of working at Beaumont, and got one a free ride home, or near there, which could be combined with a few days leave. So one fine evening, I joined a Colonel who was a doctor at the hospital, and a private as part of the escort for a mental patient being discharged from the Army under "Section 8" and sent to the veterans hospital near his home. We had Pullman reservations to and from Canandaigua, and I was assigned to sleep with the patient in a roomette. The Colonel, on his way to some leave, handed me the vouchers for the patient's meals and told me to take care of him for the two or three days it would take to get to our destination.

The young fellow seemed okay to me, and when he woke me up to go to breakfast the first morning, I gave him his breakfast voucher and rolled over and went back to sleep. Later that morning I asked the Colonel what was the matter with our patient, and he told me he was being discharged because of suicidal tendencies, so I had best keep an eye on him at all times. I gulped and didn't mention breakfast. From then on, our boy was escorted by me or the other enlisted man, but whatever depression he was having seemed to have been cured by his discharge from the Army, as he was quite happy to be going home. It was a great train trip, both ways, and the longest I would ever have. I spent the days reading, looking at the passing countryside and eating at the taxpayers' expense. We signed him over to the Veterans hospital and the three of us split for our respective homes, which in my case, I hadn't seen for about a year. I had been saving my accumulated leave to the end of my enlistment so I could get out in time for the Fall semester in college.

About this time, I began looking for a college, and applied first to Penn State, where I had assumed I would attend. My father had gone there, as well as Uncle Tom, and I had visited it a few times while in high school. The reply informed me that they would not recognize my credits from Pennsylvania Military College, and I would have to repeat the freshman year. I was having none of that: a complete waste of a year, when I still had six more years of college and law school to go. So I applied to Westminster College, which was near home, and which was happy to accept me as a transfer student. One shouldn't be surprised, but I still am in thinking how my whole life was forever changed by that small decision by Penn State, for which I shall ever be grateful. If I didn't believe in the Presbyterian doctrine of predestination then, I do now.

Towards the end of my enlistment, I got assigned to the office that was handling discharges, that is, processing the paper work to get people out of the Army. The work consisted of interviewing the soldier, and filling out the forms and the discharge papers. I got proficient enough at this that when my turn came, I discharged myself. I smile when I look at these carefully preserved documents, as I typed them myself. There was a standard interview with a colonel who asked whether we cared to reenlist, or "re-up" in Army lingo. I declined with a smile, and also resisted his suggestion that I might care to join the Army Reserves. His argument was that if we got into another war, we would all be called up anyway, and that I might be wise to preserve my sergeant's stripes. I told him if I came back, I intended to do so as an officer, not as a sergeant. That simple decision, made without much thought, kept me out of the Korean War three years later. I look back on it as a bullet missed.

Finally the happy day arrived in late August 1947. With several weeks of terminal leave, my enlistment was up, and the last thing I did was type up orders providing me with free flight home on military planes, something intended for discharged wounded veterans. It was a useful skill I had acquired while working for the discharge unit. The Army provided one with an allowance for train travel home, but I saw no point in wasting that largesse. I hitched a ride on an Air Force plane from El Paso to Mobile, and from there to Cincinnati, where I gave up on military transportation and took the train home. It had been an interesting experience, but I had seen all I wanted to see of the Army. My desire for independence had been fulfilled, and now I wanted to be independent of the Army. I wouldn't set foot on another Army base until 1990, when I went to the Army War College in Carlisle as a distinguished guest in their graduation week, but something of the Army always stays with you.

7

College Days

In about two weeks, I matriculated at Westminster as a rather disoriented sopho-more transfer student. I lived at home the first few weeks until I could find some place to stay in New Wilmington. There wasn't much dormitory space for male students then, and the Class of 1950 was the largest in the College's history, about 520 of us. In addition to the high school graduates, the class was stuffed with veterans getting out of the military services in 1946.

I elected to major in Political Science, a standard major for pre-law students. In one of the early classes, I ran into Glenn Reed, whom I had last seen fulminating at the final basketball game between East Brook and Mt. Jackson. In the mean-time, he had served a year in the Navy, and done his freshman year at Westmin-ster. I didn't know anyone else in the class, and was happy to see a face from the past. In retrospect, the previous two years had been the most impermanent part of my life, with nothing but the most transitory of relationships with other peo-ple. Now it was returning to something more normal.

Glenn was living with a half dozen other fellows in a rooming house on Waugh Avenue in New Wilmington. He told me there was a vacancy on the third floor, and suggested I try there. I did, and found a new home, rooming with three freshmen on the third floor of 420 Waugh. The rent was nominal, and now I needed only one thing more, a place to eat. Happily, some former neighbors and old friends of my parents, Mabel Gormley and her sister, Ada Stewart, and her husband, Lenza, had bought an old home in New Wilmington and were operat-ing a boarding house for students. They were kind enough to give me a job dry-ing dishes at meal times, in exchange for which I got free meals.

There was a group working there from the Alpha Sigma Phi fraternity, and one of them, Ed Drylie, was the designated dishwasher. The maitre-de and general factotum, in charge of the waiters and bill collections was Bill Bingham, who lived at our house on Waugh Avenue. Before long, the guy who had been cleaning that house moved out, and I got that job in exchange for my rent. So I had a place to live, a place to eat, and no great expenses. I had saved money while I was in the Army, maybe a couple of thousand dollars, so I didn't need to use up my GI bill. My recollection was that tuition was only about $600 for the year, which would cause any parent of today's college student to groan.

I liked the classes, with the exception of a course called "Humanities", in which I got off to a bad start. There had been an examination early on in which one was to match names and events in two parallel columns. I had known most of the answers, but misunderstood the instructions, and matched the wrong column. From there on the teacher regarded me as hopeless, and all my efforts to recover only got me back to a "C" in that course for the first semester. In everything else I got A's or B's and I never got another C in college.

At that time, attendance at chapel once a day was required, and I had to take a freshman course in Bible, which studied the Old Testament one semester, and the New in the second. I understand students at Westminster would revolt if they were required to do that now, but I have to confess I didn't mind either requirement. In chapel, we were seated alphabetically, and I sat next to an attractive girl, Helen Papazickos, who had an excellent soprano voice, and there is little a tenor likes more than singing with a good soprano. As for the Bible course, I had Wayne Christie for a teacher, and he made sure we had a thorough knowledge of that book, without which one's education would surely be lacking.

There was another required freshman course that I had to make up, and that was Speech. It was a great little course, in which you had to get up in front of the class and make a three minute speech every week or so. The teacher and the class would comment on your faults as a speaker, and while it was a little intimidating to freshman, it did help them get over their stage fright. I thought it was fun and helpful in overcoming one's amateurish faults in speaking, of which I had the usual share.

Harry Manley, the young professor in charge of the Political Science Department, was my advisor, and we got to like each other. He had an engaging grin and a friendly manner, but was one of those persons who are rather literal-minded and doesn't realize when someone is pulling his leg. Which of course students quickly find out and take advantage of. My friend, Don Wiley, a member of the class and also a pre-law student, tells me that he and his buddies were always picking on Harry, and that Glenn and I were always coming to his rescue. Harry had graduated from law school, but had not become a lawyer. Rumor had it that he had not passed the bar, but I can't confirm that. Harry later went on to become President of Muskingum College, and ended up deaning at some college out in Oregon.

I didn't have much of a social life that year. I hadn't gotten involved with any fraternity, but I had my group of friends at Mabel's and at the rooming house, and I was getting to know people in my classes. Glenn had become my closest friend, as we had similar ambitions and a prior history on which to build. He had graduated from high school with straight A's, and so far had straight A's at Westminster. I don't think this was the result of genius, he was just a thorough and conscientious student. He couldn't stand not being perfect, which seems to me to have become a great burden later on in his life. I liked to get A's, was probably equally ambitious, but did not have this obsession that I had to be perfect. In his defense, I must say that he was not just a grind: he had a warm personality, was well liked and got involved in a number of extracurricular activities, such as the debate team, at which he was a star. All in all, an interesting person, one of the most interesting I had ever met. That statement is still true today.

Glenn had a car, a 1939 Ford coupe, and when he got tired of studying, he would gather up a group of us and head out to the nearest bar, about three miles from town. New Wilmington, having been founded by United Presbyterians, was dry and alcohol was forbidden on or off campus for Westminster students. However, many of us were vets, and when we wanted a beer, we got it. The bar was known to students as the "Arm Pit", and was a tacky little concrete-walled building out in the country along route 18. But the beer and the pretzels were as good there as in Harvard Square, and we didn't mind the ambience.

Glenn had decided to take a minor in Education, as sort of an anchor to windward if he didn't become a lawyer. I thought that made sense, so I decided to do the same. That was a mistake. The courses were boring and unproductive, and I could have spent the time much more usefully. However, by the end of that school year, I felt I had to take a few summer courses to get back on track in both my major and minor, so I took some courses in June and July. That left me without a summer job, so I worked around the farm in August and joined the "52-20"

Club, which was a welfare program for vets. One could collect $20 per week for 52 weeks while looking for a job. So I must have collected eighty or a hundred bucks, and it was the last time I was on welfare until I got on Medicare at age 65.

The big political event of 1948 was the Presidential election. Glenn's Uncle Ed was a political worker in Lawrence County for the Republican party, and he told us to come to Philadelphia and he would get us into the convention. We jumped at the chance, and soon showed up at the hotel suite of Cap Rowland, the great political power of Lawrence County. I don't know which was more fun, being at the convention or hanging around the suite. The latter was a busy beehive of conspiracy and smoke filled rooms, as Cap was wheeling and dealing to swing Pennsylvania votes to Tom Dewey, which he eventually did. There really were political bosses in those days, and Cap seemed to control a lot of delegate votes.

When it came time for the climax, the voting on the candidates, there weren't enough passes to get both Glenn and me into the convention. The credentials were a badge and a written letter of authorization. Glenn generously gave me the badge, which got me through the doors without trouble, and he confronted the gatekeepers with his letter. They weren't buying his no badge stuff, so he demanded to see the person in charge of security (we knew his name from the papers). While they were looking around for him, Glenn wandered into the crowd and got lost, and soon joined me. It was much more fun sneaking in than getting there with real credentials.

Well, you may remember that young Tom Dewey, the crusading U.S. Attorney, won the nomination, beating out Harold Stassen, who had not yet become a joke, and Bob Taft. Everyone was sure that he would easily beat old Harry Truman. However, Cap kept a close eye on his parish, so that Fall he asked Glenn and me to do a house-to-house poll in a Democratic ward in New Castle, on the South Side. He thought we could pose as college students (not too difficult) and that people would be more likely to tell us than some party worker. So off we went, and the samplings were fairly gratifying to Cap, as Dewey seemed to be doing better than usual for a Republican, and the only disconcerting note was that a large number of people claimed to be undecided. The poll was taken about a week before election day, so we could hardly wait for the great triumph.

Election night finally came, and we set down with beer and pretzels to await the triumph predicted in every poll. We waited and waited, and about three in the morning I gave up and went to bed, but Glenn stayed up waiting for the rural vote to come in, which of course it never did. Against all odds, Harry Truman had won. As far as our ward on the South Side was concerned, it turned in its usual thumping Democratic majority, so all the people who were undecided had voted for Harry. While I still find elections exciting, I have learned to be wary of predictions as to the outcome.

My Junior year began in the Fall of 1948, and now I had finished most of the general education courses, and could spend more time on my major. I had been interested in Glenn's experience on the debate team, and I joined that group under the supervision of Professor Mel Moorhouse of the Speech Department. Mel was one of those wonderful teachers that can make a college education meaningful. He was witty, enjoyed being with students, loved debating and was one of those happy people who can make you feel that you are the most interesting and important person he has met lately. What a talent. So I started out debating first affirmative, where all tyros must start, as it is the easiest position. There were two people on a team, affirmative or negative, and there was an assigned debate topic for the year. That was a national assignment, so you could debate that topic anywhere, at any school. The topic for that year was "*Resolved, that a Federal World Government should be established.*" First affirmatives had to establish the need for the proposition, and then perhaps provide a general outline of the solution. I can't think I was all that good at the outset, but by the end of the year I was on the first team, with Glenn, John Kerensky, a pre-law Senior, and an experienced high school debater named Dick Stonage. We had great trips, and I remember the regional tournament at Pitt, a spring tour to William and Mary, and debating in all sorts of unusual environments, like Western Penitentiary. We debated a girls team from Chatham there, and the prisoners were much more interested in them than the topic.

Glenn and I were both invited to join the Alpha Sigma Phi fraternity, and we did. Being juniors, there wasn't much bother about fraternity hazing and initiation, and being a veteran I wasn't about to put up with any juvenile nonsense from lads younger than I. I liked the modest social life the fraternity could provide, but I didn't eat at or live in the fraternity house as I had better arrangements. Ed Drylie, my fellow dishwasher, was my fraternity father, responsible for my social education, but he bore that burden lightly. Mostly we told jokes while washing and drying dishes at Mabel's. For whatever reasons, and two years in the Army were the most likely reason, I didn't feel any great need for a fraternity, and therefore didn't get much benefit from it. I completely lost interest in it after graduation. After a year at Harvard, I decided that the undergraduate house system there made much more sense than fraternities.

Late in the summer of 1948 I decided to get a real job, as the 52-20 Club wasn't helping much, and I applied for and got a job as a part-time laborer at Sharon Steel. This was interesting, as I had never seen the inside of a steel mill before, and my first assignment was working in the bar mill. The steel ingots are heated in "soaker pits", ovens lined with brick and heated with coal and natural gas. There were dozens of them fired up on my first night there, and I was sent to shovel coal out of a railroad car and into a crane bucket. When the ingot is heated to white hot, it is lifted out of the pit by crane, and ran through the first mill, squeezing it down to a fat bar, and then through successive mills until it gets to be a slab about six inches thick, three feet wide and about fifty feet long. When the hot ingot comes out of the pit and goes into the first mill, sometimes the tail of it explodes under the pressure, sending red hot sparks flying all over the building. So this is what Dante's inferno was like. It was hot, hard work, and I was glad when that shift was over.

I worked two or three days a week, usually the 4 p.m. to 11 shift, and continued on for several months while I was in school. I stayed at the bar mill, but mostly worked outdoors, loading the slabs onto railroad cars. I can't say I learned a whole lot about making steel, but I got to know the workers and could understand a little of their life. There was one old Hungarian named Mike who would show me what to do, and I liked him for that. He was an immigrant and his English wasn't too good, but good enough for this. Shortly before the election, I asked him what he thought of it. His reply was "If Hoover come, we no wash hands." I had to have some help translating this, but what he meant was that if a Republican got elected, the men would not be allowed to wash up on Company time, as this was a right obtained during Roosevelt's term. I didn't think much of his analysis, but that didn't matter, he knew how he was going to vote. Well, Hoover didn't come, so Mike kept on washing up on Company time. That is, until the entire steel industry collapsed about thirty years later, under the weight of high wages and obsolete equipment. Sharon Steel went into bankruptcy several years ago.

I didn't continue on at Sharon Steel after my junior year, as I couldn't handle the hours and the classes, but I have always been grateful for the experience, plus the money, which got me through that year of college. I didn't have to join the United Steelworkers Union, as I was only a part-timer, but later I was sorry I hadn't. It would have looked interesting in the resume of a corporate director. When I got to my senior year thesis, I wrote on the political and economic agenda of the C.I.O., of which the U.S.W. was a major part, and that turned out to be an interesting subject. I got an "A" for that effort. When I was practicing law in my younger years, I used to keep a picture of a steel mill hanging in my office: when I got tired and frustrated with what I was doing, it was a mute reminder that life was a whole lot harder working in a steel mill. That, and hauling hay, have been great incentives for me to avoid hard work.

In the Summer after my Junior year, I followed Glenn's example from the previous Summer, and got a job with a New Wilmington contractor, Vic Minteer. Vic had been in the Army with my dad, so he knew my origins. He had a modest business doing highway work, general contracting and whatever came along. My first job was painting the oil storage tanks belonging to Phil Campbell, who owned the lumber store, an oil distribution business and a concrete mixing plant in New Wilmington. The oil tanks were easy, but then I had to move on to the underside of the ramp to the concrete batch plant. That went up to about eighty feet above the ground, so to paint the steel girders holding it up one had to work from a platform slung underneath the girders and nothing but air underneath. One hand for yourself, and one for the brush. I got over any fear of heights that summer. I worked for Vic that summer and for the next three Summers, and will always be indebted to him for the jobs, the money and the experience.

My senior year at Westminster was largely devoted to my major, my thesis, debating, and a whole new interest that developed during that year. At an early meeting of the debate team, Mel Moorehouse introduced me to two new members of the team, both sophomore women. He told us that I would be their mentor. One of these girls was named Virginia Reehl, which I thought was memorable, but not knowing what was expected in my new role, I merely said hello, and went back to my conversation with my new partner, Frank Jones.

One would think when encountering such a Moment of Predestination, there would be some Divine whisper, nudge in the ribs, a wink, something that would say "*This is your Future!*" Nope. Maybe my receiver was not turned on. In any event, I thought no more about my role as mentor for several weeks. Later that Fall, Glenn and I had to go into Pittsburgh to take the Law School Aptitude Test,

a standard test relied on heavily by law schools in making their application accep-
tances. It was a long, intense day, and on the way home we stopped for dinner at
the old Kaufman Hotel in Zelienople. Who did we find there but the women's
debate team on their way home from some debate. This time I took a good look
at Virginia, noticed her beautiful eyes, lovely face, and yes, well-developed figure.
Perhaps I should be paying a little more attention to her progress. Yes.

I must have begun teaching her everything I knew about debate, for not long
after that she invited me to a sorority party. We went to the movie house in New
Wilmington, where Alec Guiness was playing in "The Lavendar Hill Mob", and
afterwards to the sorority house. Not only was she beautiful, she was fun! Amaz-
ing! Yes, children, I got a warm good-night kiss on our first date.

I was a little deflated later when I learned that she had invited me to the party as
the result of a bet with the other women debaters. They thought I wouldn't go,
because I was too serious about law school, didn't like women or whatever. Ginnie took on the challenge, and thought up answers to every excuse I could make
to avoid going to the party. Oh well, she won the bet, and if there was any argument about it, she won that too. I don't believe I have won an argument with her
since then, which shows what a good debate coach I was.

Eventually, the LSAT scores were announced, and mine were good enough to get
me into all the law schools to which I had applied, which were Harvard, Michigan, Penn and Pitt. Glenn had the same experience, and so we both chose Harvard Law School, naturally. We had gotten the Harvard inspiration from Tom
Mansell, a lawyer then practicing in New Castle, who lived down the street on
Waugh Avenue from us. Tom was a Westminster and Harvard Law School graduate, and was teaching a senior course on Constitutional Law. It was a great
course for preparing one for law school, as he followed the same "case study"
method in use there. I have often told Tom that he was responsible for getting me
into Harvard, for getting me onto the Law Review, and for my doing poorly in
Con Law in law school. He was responsible for getting us into Harvard since we
figured that if he could get in, we should be able to do the same. He got credit for
my doing well the first year because having a college year on the case method gave
me a leg up on that first year. And I didn't do too well in Con Law at Harvard
because I found the material repetitious and boring, so that was Tom's fault.

Looking back on my college life, I don't have too many regrets. I think a small college was right for me at the time. If I could change it, I wouldn't have taken the education courses, and I would have taken some in economics. I wish I had gone back and taken calculus again, and I could have used a course in statistics. I should have devoted some time to music, at least in singing in the college choir, and it would have been a great time to take voice lessons. A course in botany would have been interesting in later life as well. Well, I didn't and I have had to make up for those deficiencies later in life. The one great thing that Westminster did do for me was to leave me with a desire for learning that has lasted all my life, and one can't expect much more from a college education. And we need not speak of certain relationships formed there.

But, speaking of that, I had more dates with Ginnie that last semester, and by the end of that year we were dating pretty regularly. I was smitten with her, and she seemed to like me more than a little, although I couldn't understand why. There was one little problem in the background. She had another boyfriend at Annapolis, and he was graduating that year also. She had been to a dance at the Naval Academy with him, but I had the advantage of being in New Wilmington. She finished her exams a week or so before graduation, and went home to New Brighton, but said she would come back to see me graduate.

The day of graduation finally came, and Glenn finished first in the class, of course, with straight "A"s, the first ever in the history of the College. I graduated *magna cum laude*, having carefully avoided the pitfall of perfection. I don't remember who the Commencement speaker was, but one memory is printed indelibly on my brain. I was sitting on the terrace outside Old Main, where commencement exercises are always held in fair weather, and the day was warm and sunny. It was in the middle of the proceedings when I spotted Ginnie, but she was on the arm of a white-uniformed naval officer! My heart sank, as that seemed to be the answer to the question of which boyfriend had won the day. My last day at Westminster went downhill from there, and I didn't try to find her after the graduation ceremony was finished.

I went back to work for Vic Minteer that summer, working on various small bridge projects for the highway department, and tried to pretend that my lost love didn't matter. Then events took an unexpected turn. I got a letter from Ginnie apologizing for having shown up at graduation with a certain Naval Person, and asked if I would be willing to pick her up at the train station in New Castle and take her home from there. I don't remember what trip brought her to New Castle. She still seemed interested in me, and it didn't take me long to swallow my injured pride and accept the offer.

What a happy reunion that was! It was boy meets girl, boy loses girl, boy wins back girl! The stuff of movies. She wanted me to meet her parents, who were curious about me but properly reserved in any enthusiasm for this new boyfriend of their only daughter. (I think they liked the guy in the Navy; he at least had a job.) So I took her home, and met Wiibur and Ethel Reehl, and none of our lives has been the same since.

A word about this couple destined to be my in-laws. Wib, as he was known. was then in his mid-forties, and Ethel a little younger. He had worked all his life for American Bridge Division of U.S. Steel, as an engineer-draftsman, as had his father before him. He was a vigorous, friendly, extroverted man, then in the prime of life, but he smoked too much. He was the president of the local Lions Club, and had gone on to higher things with the Lions at the state level. He once told me that he wished he had gone into sales, and he would have been a natural as a salesman. He had been an expert bridge player, but had given up competitive play a few years before I met him.

Ethel was the musician in the family, and had sung in a quartet at the Beaver Presbyterian Church to help put Ginnie through college. She was a talented piano player, and much in demand for accompanying groups like the Lions. She could play any tune, with or without music. Her health had been a bit more frail, and she had no more children after Ginnie was born. Her parents, John and Molly Huff lived next door to them, and Wib's mother lived across the street (his father died while Ginnie was in college). Thus Ginnie had been not only an "only child", but had grown up surrounded by doting grandparents. Obviously my work was cut out for me.

I think Ginnie met my parents some time that summer of 1950. If my reception was cool, her's was downright hostile, at least on the part of my mother. I guess she thought this slick woman from the city (well, New Brighton may have seemed like the city to a woman who had spent her life on a farm) was a danger-ous threat to her innocent Robby. I thought Ginnie showed remarkable aplomb in not letting this reaction bother her, and her patience with my mother for many years since has been a tribute to her character. (She hasn't been nearly as patient with me).

Once we got started, we continued dating that summer, but September came and I had to leave for Cambridge. We had one last date, going to a play in Pittsburgh the night before I was to leave. I was driving my Dad's 1950 Packard, only a few months old, as I didn't have a car to call my own then, and there was a long and poignant farewell when I took Ginnie home. It was raining quite hard when I left her house about midnight, and I hadn't gotten a mile from there when I put on the brakes coming to a sharp curve and the car slid straight ahead, coming to rest against a telephone pole. The front end was smashed, but I wasn't hurt, and this was long before seat belts. That was one of the lower points of my life. Wib came to rescue me, and I stayed at their house overnight until I could get the car towed to New Castle in the morning. Dad didn't say a word, and the car eventually got fixed. He did replace the tires, as he also found that they didn't do well on wet pavement.

Glenn drove the two of us to Cambridge in his Ford, with me in a rather crest-fallen mood after the accident, and I think we did it in one day, a long drive even by today's standards.

8

The Law School

Harvard Law School had just built a new set of dormitories and a commons building, all designed by Walter Gropius in the modern style of the Bauhaus movement. They looked quite striking, but weren't very well suited to quiet living. Some architects think more about appearances than the comfort of the occupants. However, Glenn and I got the end room in Story Hall, first floor, nearest to the Commons and Langdell Hall, the main class room and library building. The room had nice large windows, and single beds arranged against the end walls, with desks in the middle. The beds doubled as sofas during the day. There wasn't room for any other furniture. It didn't matter as we were soon into the monastic life of first year law students.

I won't try to describe that life in detail. That has been done in Scott Turow's "*1L*", and somewhat frivolously in the movie "*Paper Chase*". It was exciting as well as competitive, and I never studied harder in my life. There were about 500 of us starting out in the class, but we lost about 100 that year to the Korean War, mostly reservists. I escaped by reason of my eighteen-months service in the Regular Army, and not having joined the Reserves just to keep my sergeant's stripes.

Classes were large, as each of us was assigned to a section with about 125 students, and we went to all of our classes with that group. Glenn and I were in different sections, so we had different professors, and often different case books. The school encouraged study in small groups, so I got together with four others from my section, and we met for a few hours each week to talk and argue about what we thought we were learning. They were all good students (which was true of just about everybody in the class) and I enjoyed our sessions. The oldest was, appropriately, Ollie Oldman, who later became a professor of international taxation at Harvard. He and Bob Shults, of Arkansas, were both married veterans. Hugo Melvoin of Chicago was a newly-wed, and Bob Huntington, of Oregon, and I, the two bachelors, made up the rest of the study group. Of all of these, the only one I have not stayed in touch with is Bob Huntington, who hasn't come back to any reunions. They were and are all great people, and I would give a lot to be able to sit down and reminisce with them about that first year.

Somehow we found a little time to see some of the sights of Boston. Glenn and I drove out to Walden Pond, Lexington and Concord one fine fall day. We could catch the subway at Harvard Square and ride into Boston, with the Boston Gardens and the swan boats. I tried to keep up some physical exercise, and joined a volleyball group at Heminway gym. I was playing there one November afternoon when I came down on my right foot the wrong way, and cracked the little toe bone in my foot. Nobody ever accused me of being an athlete. The orthopedic surgeon taped it up and sent me to a shoemaker to have a steel plate put in my shoe. I spent a few weeks on crutches, not at a good time. We had a hurricane as Thanksgiving approached, and there is nothing like walking on crutches in a 90 mile-an-hour wind. That same storm dumped three feet of snow on Western Pennsylvania, and I have been hearing those snow stories ever since.

One of our friends and classmates, Austin B. Noble, whose name is a complete hortatory sentence, invited Glenn and me to his parents' home in Royalton, Vermont for Thanksgiving. It was a glorious New England experience: the weather was cold and there was about a foot of snow on the ground. We had a great feast and I remember standing outside in the cold air that night thinking I had never heard more complete silence than in that country home outside a small town in Vermont. I was still on crutches, but I felt very much at home in that rural setting.

Glenn and I had one fellow sufferer from home that year. My Uncle Tom, Dad's younger brother, was getting his Master's degree in Public Administration at Littauer Center at Harvard. He had been out of college for about twenty years, and I think he worried more about getting through than we did. He and Aunt Margaret, his first wife who died several years later, had a little apartment not far from the Law School, and from time to time they would have us out for a home-cooked dinner and mutual anxiety session. I had not known him very well as I was growing up, but we got to know each other that winter and remained good friends until his death a few years ago at age 92.

Christmas resulted in vacation and a trip home, and I spent much of my time with Ginnie, with whom I now had no doubt of being head-over-heels. We had corresponded nearly daily while I was in Cambridge. I was getting to know her family better, and her grandparents, Lyla Reehl, known as Mema, and John and Molly Huff, *alias dictus* Grandpa and Grandma, warmly accepted me into the group. Her parents were lively and fun to be with, and if they viewed me with some skepticism it would be understandable. I have had daughters of that age myself.

Part of the stress generated at Harvard Law School arose from the fact that one studied the entire first year without receiving any grades, and everything turns on the final exams in May. To alleviate this sense of "*I don't know how I'm doing*" the school has a tutorial program with about a dozen students in each, lead by a teaching assistant. It was a good program, and had practice exams to help people learn how to answer essay questions. We never had any other kind of exam, and I never saw a true-false or multiple choice test while we were there. I still consider the essay exam the only reliable test of a student.

Another feature of the first year is the Ames competition. These are moot court appellate arguments, with about eight students in a "club" competing against other clubs. In the first year, two-man teams argue against each other, *mano a mano*, giving everybody a chance at oral argument. The cases are interesting and difficult, and each team has to write a brief and then argue their side before a three-person court, which consists of three third-year students for the first round.

Subsequent rounds in the second and third year involve the entire club, each competing against another eight-person club. Finally, the final round for the winners of the preliminary events occurs, with the judges being three Federal Court judges, one of them from the Supreme Court.

Getting back to that first round, I had the good fortune to be teamed up with Ian Macneil, a graduate of the University of Vermont. He had an unusual background: his mother had died some years before, and he had been raised by his father, an architect in Boston. His father had a title, "The Macneil", as he was head of the Macneil of Barra clan of Scotland. He owned the family castle on the island of Barra, the southernmost island of the Outer Hebrides. Many years later we would visit that lovely place.

Ian was a delight to work with: his mind seemed to work like mine; he had a great sense of humor, and we amused each other no end. There was a preliminary round in which we argued against each other, and I recall that I won that argument, but it was close. Then we paired up to argue the second round against another two-man team. We wrote our brief for our Ames case (I don't now remember anything about the case, except it was a nicely drawn moot case with some developing precedent in the courts). We went to the oral argument with some nervous anticipation, but the argument went very well. We not only won our case, we were given a prize for the best oral argument in the entire first year class! We each received a book, "*Selected Writings of Benjamin Nathan Cardozo*" with a bookplate inside commemorating our victory. I still have the book today, and treasure it for that happy memory. For reasons we will get to, that was the end of my participation in the Ames Competition, as well as Ian's.

It is probably not surprising that this old debater enjoyed oral argument, and the few occasions when I got to argue before an appellate court in my professional life were always red-letter days in my life. There's nothing like the fun of the give-and-take of oral argument.

I had some great professors that year. Warren Seavey for Torts was the classic Socratic teacher. He refused to express any principle of law, and any he elucidated from his students he systematically destroyed under cross-examination. It is a wonderful method to make students think for themselves. He had a trick of saying to a student who put up his hand to offer some new insight into the discussion "*And you were about to say….*" going on to state what the student was about to say. I thought it was just a trick until one day I put up my hand, and he said "*And you were about to say….*" and went on with exactly what I had intended to say. It left me with the uncanny feeling that he could read one's mind. I think he had been teaching so long (he was in his late 60's) he knew exactly where every classroom discussion was headed, and enjoyed anticipating it.

I also had Lon Fuller for Contracts, and I realized when I took his second year course in Jurisprudence (legal philosophy) that he had been teaching us philosophy the entire first year in Contracts, a subject that lends itself well to philosophic thought. Though I get ahead of my story, Ian went on to become a renowned professor of Contracts, and he once told me that his philosophy of contracts had originated with Fuller but he had kept going where Fuller stopped, which is typical Macneil modesty.

My other professors were good, but not in the class of Giants like Seavey and Fuller. Great teachers not only teach the subject matter, they shape your mind with attitudes and values that last for life.

Well, the year wore on, with the first year students beginning to "think like lawyers", and nervously anticipating the great reckoning. The exams began in late May, and my first was Torts. I had a hard time getting to sleep the night before. The exams were about three hours long, consisting of a few hypothetical situations to which one wrote essay type answers. I chose to write in long-hand, although one could type if one wished (the typists were sent to their own noisy room). I just felt more comfortable thinking while writing rather than typing. Computers and word processing hadn't been invented.

Soon the last test was over, and Glenn and I drove home. We both had jobs with Vic Minteer that summer, working on road construction projects such as building small bridges or culverts and the like. The work was hard, but paid well by my standards. Any free evening I could get was spent driving down to New Brighton to see Ginnie, where she was working as a counselor at a school playground.

Ian Macneil got called up in the Reserves, so that was the last I was to see of him in Law School. He got out of the Army two years later, and came back and finished with the Class of 1955.

Toward the end of June a letter arrived in the mail from Cambridge with the results of the first year. I had passed! Even more astounding, I had finished ninth in the class, and therefore was elected to the Law Review, which was limited to the top twenty in the class. Glenn had done well, finishing in the top 10%, and became a member of the student board that provided free legal services to indigents. Ian had also gotten on the Law Review, but the Army had better uses for him.

I must have been in a state of pleasant confusion for a few days. Law Review was just not something I had ever thought about. I knew that it practically guaranteed a job in any large law firm that I would choose, provided I could keep my grades up enough to stay on for my last year. We were advised that we would have to spend a minimum of forty hours a week doing research, writing and editing for the Review, in addition to going to law school, and that we were expected to report by the end of August, several weeks in advance of the start of classes. Several hundred pages of advance sheets arrived in the mail so I could get started on the reading.

So the rest of the summer flew by. Near the end, I went out to dinner with Ginnie one evening and gave her my fraternity pin, and we agreed that we would get engaged in December. Getting "pinned" seems a little sophomoric now, but she was starting her senior year at Westminster and it meant something to her to have some status with my former fraternity. And what it meant to me was that I knew who my future bride would be, and I couldn't have been happier.

9

The Law Review

So back to Cambridge in the last week of August, to learn what it was like to be an editor of the Harvard Law Review, the grandfather of scores of other student law reviews, and to find a place to live. I didn't want another year in the dormitories, I just wanted some quiet place without a lot of people. I got acquainted with one of my fellow editors, Marty Richman, who was also looking for a home, and we teamed up to rent two rooms in a private home on Garden Street, a few blocks from the law school, just opposite from Radcliffe. The couple that lived there were retired, and the home was the quiet haven we both wanted. But my good fortune was finding Marty, a quiet but brilliant student, who became a good friend and has remained one for all the years since then.

The junior editors were naturally assigned the grunt work of the Review. Reading advance sheets to find interesting cases to review, cite-checking articles submitted by professors and scholars for publication, and eventually being assigned a case for which to write a case note. Hours spent in the library were rewarded by getting to know my fellow editors. Most had been in other sections in the first year and were strangers, but I soon got to know them and couldn't have picked more enjoyable company. Wayne Barnett had been first in the class that year: a mathematics major from Harvard, first in his class there as well. Gerry Gunther had come in second, and he was the old man of the group. A protege of Felix Frankfurter at Columbia, he had already had a career in teaching. Jack Kevorkian was an engaging Philadelphian, his father an immigrant from Armenia who had been the only survivor of his village following the Turkish massacre. Randy Warner was from Arkansas, and through him I got to know his roommate Bill Swanson, from Pittsburgh. It took us some time to learn that when Randy said he had gone to school in "Fedville", that the home of his alma mater was spelled "Fayetteville". He taught us all how to call the hogs, which if you didn't know, is the war cry of the Razorbacks of the University of Arkansas.

The luxury of no classes for the first few weeks soon ended, and there we were with the full schedule of classes and still spending our 40 hours on the Review. It was a struggle to keep up with the class work, and one recurring nightmare for many years was about walking into an exam without ever having read the material or attended the classes. And second year classes weren't quite as exciting as the first year. We had constitutional law, which I had had in college, and accounting for lawyers, and I had taken a college course in accounting. Corporation law might have been interesting, but wasn't. Federal income tax was a taste of the real world, but I didn't have Erwin Griswold, who was the star of that show, as a teacher. Somehow class work didn't seem as interesting as the Law Review, which always claimed a higher priority. The teachers of that year just didn't measure up to the quality of the first year, and later, those of the third year.

I was assigned to write up a recent case for the Review. Recent Cases are student written analyses of interesting cases, usually about a page or less in print. I learned from that the thoroughness of the editing process. After one had written one of these terse gems, a third year editor would go over it and convince you that just about every word written could be improved upon. After that process, which resulted in a completely new version, you had to defend that to the editor in charge of Recent Cases, who would usually throw out everything from that draft. I think what it taught was that no written sentence is ever perfect and can always be made more succinct, and that one had better be prepared to defend vigorously every written word, comma and quotation. God forbid that any of the citations would be incorrect, because someone else would be checking those.

Christmas was the big event of the year. As promised in the summer vacation, I arrived at home with an engagement ring, which Hugo Melvoin had helped me purchase, knowing that I was an innocent when it came to buying diamonds. It was small, which was all that I could afford, but Ginnie was pleased with it and has worn it ever since, spurning all diamond rings of larger caliber, to her great credit. I presented it on Christmas Eve, and when we went to the midnight church service, she kept glancing admiringly at her left hand.

Then the painful parting and back to school, and in the flurry of work the year went by and summer came again. It turned out that I hadn't done quite so well the second year, but good enough to stay on the Law Review. I did only average in Con Law and Accounting, the two subjects that were most familiar from college, and got my worst grade in law school in Corporations. Lousy teacher was my excuse. Lack of attention to the material was the real reason for all of them. I later concluded that the grade in Corp. Law was the reason I graduated *cum laude* instead of *magna cum laude* and was belatedly grateful for it. The former was a sufficient burden to bear in the practice of law, and the latter might have ruined me.

10

Married Life

Comes the summer of 1952, and I am back working for Vic Minteer, this time on the "new" science building at Westminster, one which has been completely replaced since I have been a trustee of that institution, but that gets far ahead of the story. There is one big event looming for this summer: Ginnie and I are to be married on August 15. There were all the plans for the wedding, with respect to which the prospective groom is largely a spectator, however essential he may be as a participant.

That summer wore me down, and about a week or so before the big event I quit the job just to get a little rest. In my state of torpor, I must not have been showing great excitement about the wedding, which caused my prospective mother-in-law to question me as to whether I really wanted to get married. The answer was "yes". And so we did.

The event was on August 15, at the New Brighton Methodist Church, which had been attended by Ginnie, her parents and grandparents for many years. Her grandfather Dempsey Reehl had been the Sunday School Superintendent there, and the church remains a significant space in our lives. The wedding was in the evening, at 7:30 as I recall, and it was a hot and muggy summer evening. Glenn was my best man, of course, and Austin Noble and Bill Swanson were ushers. Austin had driven from Vermont, and it was the first time he had been out of New England.

The reception was in the church basement, which was fine for both our parents. My mother would have been shocked by a reception at which alcohol was served. We drove from there to Pittsburgh, and spent our first night of married life at the William Penn Hotel, which was hosting a convention of firemen that night. They didn't keep us up.

We did a little shopping in Pittsburgh the next day, as Ginnie needed to buy a pair of stockings. We got into a discussion about which of us would pay for them, and I reminded her that it didn't make much difference now. We drove down to Uniontown, where we spent the next two nights at the old Summit Inn, atop Chestnut Ridge. Then we drove back to New Castle and New Brighton and packed up for our trip to Cambridge.

We drove via Erie and across New York State, staying overnight in the Finger Lakes area. We were driving my old 1939 Plymouth, which leaked water from the radiator, but it survived the trip. It was warm, and I remember Ginnie was wearing heels that sunk into the rubber mat on the floor. In the course of two days, we arrived in Cambridge, homeless, jobless and broke.

That experience taught me a valuable lesson: in the face of adversity, my new wife was cheerful and resolute. We soon found an apartment on Dana Street, with an Irish landlord couple, the Youngs, who quickly took us under their wing. I had a little trouble in communication at first. When Mrs. Young asked me my name, I answered "Patton", and she wrote down "Pattern". I then spelled the name, and she said "Oh, Pattern" and promptly spelled out "Patton." So do we speak in Cambridge.

It was a charming house, with a green lawn in front and a gravel path, and we shared the second floor and bathroom with another student couple, the Scotts. They both were graduate students, in the English department, I believe, and hopeless liberals. We had nothing in common, politically or intellectually, as they were followers of Henry Agard Wallace, that leftist fool from the Roosevelt administration, and we were loyal Republicans supporting Dwight Eisenhower. Of course, they saw no hope for those servants of capitalism, the lawyers. They firmly believed that if the impossible happened, and Eisenhower were elected, the country would proceed directly to Fascism. I described them, in private, as "Scotts wha hae with Wallace bled." Perhaps it was best that way, as neither of us bothered the other, finding each other such unlikely neighbors. I have since wondered whether they survived the Reagan years.

Ginnie had searched in vain for a teaching job in the Boston area, but not surprisingly the authorities had little interest in a mid-western Protestant wife whose husband had one year left in law school. But happily she found a job as a bookkeeper with a little Cambridge company called "Baird Associates" which was one of the early high-techs of that area. She had not had any accounting, and the first night after starting her new job she asked me whether debits were good and credits were bad, or was it the other way around. We dispensed with that idea, and the next day she established that debits were next to the door, and credits next to the window, which was enough for that job. Happily her boss, Diane Pearson, was a CPA wife of a Business School student, and we became friends with them, and I'm happy to say, still are. Diane and Larry Pearson returned to the Pacific Northwest, and he had a distinguished career with Weyerhauser in Vancouver. Diane was small in size, and had collected money from large football players while in college by betting she could drink a bottle of beer faster than they could. She always won, because she had the ability to keep her epiglottis closed without swallowing, and could pour down any liquid without stopping. It is a strange accomplishment, but useful.

Ginnie's job paid the handsome sum of $40 per week, and with a loan of $600 from the law school (interest free, pay it back when you can) we financed my third year at Harvard. We could barely get through each week financially, but we did, and it is probably the best way to start married life. I doubt we would have been any happier if we had had no financial worries. I was working night and day, between law school and the Review, so free time was rare. We did manage to afford a 1/6 interest in two season tickets to the Boston Symphony, shared with other members of the Review, and those were our big nights out.

Glenn developed stomach ulcer problems that year, and asked if he could eat dinner with us from time to time, to keep to some sensible diet. He did, and he provided his own groceries, which often looked better than what we were eating. The most memorable meal that I remember was on Thanksgiving Day, when Ginnie roasted a turkey with all the trimmings, and we had Glenn and Austin as guests. I think we even had a bottle of white wine.

I had great courses at school that year, with Jim Casner in Estate Planning, Paul Freund in Conflicts of Law, and best of all, I got into Paul Freund's seminar on Constitutional Litigation. It is hard to describe the pleasure and excitement in having a great teacher, but Freund was the best I ever had: wise, witty, experienced and charming, it was always a privilege to be around him.

I was writing a note for the "Notes" section of the Harvard Law Review that year on the subject of state anti-communist statutes. This period was the high-water mark of McCarthyism and many states had adopted laws requiring registration of communists and other restrictions, as had the Federal government. The subject of my note was whether the state statutes had been superseded by the Federal law under the constitutional doctrine of "occupation of the field" by the Federal government. There was no precedent in this area and the result if the question were ever raised was far from clear. Happily, I could use my research on this to satisfy my thesis requirements for the Con Law litigation seminar.

My note and paper did not draw any conclusion as to how the Supreme Court would decide the issue if it ever got it. When we discussed my paper in the seminar, Paul Freund asked at the conclusion what my opinion was as to how the Court might rule. I told him I didn't know, and added I would leave that to those who understood the Supreme Court. That was a mild jape, as Paul had written a well known book entitled "On Understanding the Supreme Court". Since then I have often wondered whether I should have hazarded a guess on the outcome.

The question was answered several years later when the U.S. Supreme Court got that issue in the Nelson case, and found that the Pennsylvania statute was precluded by the Federal statute (*Pennsylvania v Nelson*, 350 U.S. 497 (1956)). I was pleased that the opinion cited my note in the Harvard Law Review (footnote 4, p.514). Now for a real coincidence: when Nelson (and the communist party) were taking their case to the Pennsylvania Supreme Court, they asked John Buchanan if he would represent them. I was then an associate in his office, and he asked me the same question that Paul Freund had asked. I gave him the same answer: I didn't know, and the question was so close nobody could know until the Court enlightened us. For whatever reason, he decided he did not want to represent Nelson, to my regret, as I could then have used my research a third time in the brief to the Supreme Court.

The other course I particularly enjoyed that year was Jim Casner's course in estate planning. Probably no course in law school was of as much practical use to me over my years of practice as that one. Casner was a master of the subject and a great teacher. I have been asked whether he was the model for the law school professor in the movie "*Paper Chase*". I thought not: Casner was much more entertaining, although he was an acerbic, quick-witted debater who greatly relished making a student look like a fool, as the fictional character did.

A third year experience was job-hunting. At that time, law firms hadn't started to recruit second year students for summer jobs, as they do now, so the recruiting took place in the fall of the third year. Most large firms came to campus, and like my brethren, I talked to most of the firms in cities where I might like to practice. The Law Review was a ticket to most of them, so I had two choices: where did I want to go, and with whom. I considered Boston, Philadelphia, New York, Cleveland and Pittsburgh. After some flirtations with the other cities, I finally decided on Pittsburgh. Our families were near, I had lived in Western Pennsylvania all my life, and I liked the law firms there. I talked to Reed Smith Shaw & McClay; Kirkpatrick Pomeroy Lockhart & Johnson; and Smith Buchanan Ingersoll Rodewald & Eckert. Firms didn't go in for short snappy names then. I liked both of the latter two, and spent time with both over the Christmas holiday.

Paul Rodewald was in charge of recruiting for Smith Buchanan and was the father of my classmate and fellow Law Reviewer, Bill. Obviously, Bill was joining that firm. Also Glenn Reed got an offer from them that he accepted. They had new offices in the Alcoa Building, just finished, and had a higher starting salary than Kirkpatrick's firm. It was the magnificent sum of $4,800 per year, which is much less than the monthly salary law firms now pay. But at that time it was regarded as a good salary for first year associates. So I joined Bill and Glenn and accepted their offer.

It was 1953, I was twenty-five years old, and in the previous five years I had decided on a career, a law school, a wife and the law firm I was to join. It occurred to me that I had made most of the major decisions of my life, and in retrospect, they all seemed like good choices, but the choice of a wife was the best and most enduring. It would be hard for me not to believe in predestination, and that a Divine hand had been placed on my shoulder.

The school year came to a close, and I was ready to go to work and needed the money, so I started at Smith Buchanan on June 1, even though I still had the bar examination to take.

11

Lawyering

Graduation from Law School was in early June, but I decided to skip it, as it would have been expensive to go back and we were broke. I think my parents were a little disappointed, and I am sorry about that, as it would have been their one chance to see Cambridge and Fair Harvard. Somehow the ceremony didn't seem significant to me, and the prospects of working and taking the bar exam were excitement enough. We also had to find a place to live, and thought that the suburb of Mt. Lebanon was about our style, so we found a one-bedroom apartment on the corner of Castle Shannon Boulevard and Shady Drive East. My father-in-law lent us some money to get started, as we didn't have a dime. We bought a few pieces of furniture, got a few hand-me-downs from family, and we had our new home.

I started to work at the firm on June 1, and arranged to take the bar exam cram course which was given in the evening. It was held in the old Roosevelt Hotel on Sixth Street, and most of the people expecting to take the exam in Pittsburgh were there. So the summer was spent working during the days, going to class in the evenings, and studying the outlines provided by the cram course whenever time permitted. Ginnie started job-hunting when we were settled in, and found a job teaching in the elementary school in Brentwood that Fall. They had a prejudice against hiring married teachers, and she solemnly promised the superintendent that she intended to work for at least two years before we planned to begin a family. The superintendent was a family friend from New Brighton, and she got the job, becoming the first married teacher hired in Brentwood.

June and July went by in that fashion. My work at the firm was light, mostly research in the library. The partners knew I had the bar exam ahead of me, and suggested I give first priority to it.

The big day, or rather two days, came at the end of July. The bar exam was given at Pitt Law School, which was then high in the Tower of Learning. A far cry from the vastness of Harvard, and hot as Hades in the Summer heat. The exam was of the essay question type, just as we had in law school. That has since been replaced in part by a multiple-choice test, which is easy to grade but doesn't measure much of the stuff you learn in law school. As usual, I didn't have any idea how I had done, but don't recall any anxiety about it.

To cut to the chase, we didn't get the results until November. I got on the trolley one Monday morning and sat down to read the Post-Gazette. There on a back page was a list of "local residents" who had passed the bar. My name was not on it. Glenn's name was, as well as the names of my Pittsburgh friends and classmates. The paper slid off my lap. What a disaster! I, an editor of the Harvard Law Review with a job in a prestigious law firm, had I flunked the bar? There was one chance that I hadn't. I had originally registered in Lawrence County, and maybe I wasn't a "local resident". That seemed like a slim chance, as Glenn had also registered in Lawrence County. But the office of the Pittsburgh Legal Journal was just across the Smithfield Bridge, and I decided not to jump off it until I had seen if they had the complete list for the state. I stopped there before going to my office, and yes, they had the list, and I immediately turned to Lawrence County. There, in solitary splendor, was my name. Why my name was there, and Glenn's in Allegheny County, we never could figure out.

Well, I proceeded to the office feeling much relieved. Glenn was waiting at the reception desk with a worried look, holding the morning paper. I told him to quit worrying, of course I had passed the Bar. He had gotten the paper on Sunday evening, and after conferring with my friends, decided not to call me that evening with the bad news. I thanked him for that. I stopped in at Paul Rodewald's office to give him the good news, and he had heard from Don McCaskey, my preceptor, that my name had not been in the paper. He said to me "Let's have a little fun with Don." He picked up the phone, called him and said "Don't worry about Patton, I'll take care of it" and hung up. Then he told me to go straight to Don's office and tell him I had just passed. He was laughing as I went out, but I was still too shaken to be ready to laugh.

I called Ginnie's school with the news, and shortly after all this I had a call from my mother. She had received an official looking letter from the Bar Examiners addressed to me. I asked her to open it, and she read it. Guess what: I had passed the bar examination. If they could have found a less torturous way of letting me know I would have appreciated it.

The firm threw an impromptu party at the Harvard-Yale-Princeton Club that evening to celebrate with the soon-to-be admitted lawyers. I had the unique advantage in that I could tell them what it felt like to flunk the bar and pass it on the same day. The story was told and retold every year after that at similar celebrations.

Going back to the summer after the bar exam, a few significant events took place. In early September, when she had been at work for only a few weeks, Ginnie began to feel ill, and consulted a doctor. He told her she was fine, just a little pregnant. What a dilemma: she had promised that she would be available as a teacher for a minimum of two years. With tears and trepidation, she had to inform the superintendent who had hired her. He took the news with good grace, but we suspected with an unspoken resolve that he would never hire a married female teacher again. Needless to say, the prospect of a new family member was one of the things on my mind the day of that fateful trolley ride when I thought I had flunked the Bar.

The first real case I was asked to work on was with Bill Eckert, the senior trial lawyer of the firm, and Frank Seamans, a younger partner known universally as "Zeke". An elderly farmer named James Brookbank owned a farm in Cameron County, in the mountains to the notheast of Pittsburgh. He leased his gas drilling rights to the B & M Oil and Gas Company, which drilled a well that proved to be quite a good gas well. There was a railroad right-of-way running through the farm, and the Benedum Trees Oil Company went to the owner of the railroad (the B & O Railroad) and got a lease from it. Benedum then drilled a well close to Mr. Brookbank's well, and it was even better. Neither Mr. Brookbank nor B & M thought highly of this, as they didn't think the railroad had any right to the gas. So they sued, and their lawyers came to Bill Eckert for help on the case.

The question of who owned the gas under the right-of-way turned on a written instrument dated in 1903 between some people named Ingraham, who were Mr. Brookbank's predecessors in title to the farm, and the Susquehanna and Southern Railroad, which merged into the B & O many years later. It was an interesting document, on a printed form of the railroad, and recited that the Ingrahams, for $300, "have granted, bargained, sold, released and conveyed" to the Susquehanna

& Southern a strip of land four rods in width, one-half on each side of center line "as now located" of the S & S Railroad. In the second paragraph, the document gave the railroad the right to lay out, construct, maintain and operate a railroad on the land, and released it from all liability therefor. In the notarized acknowledgement, the Ingrahams acknowledged the "foregoing release" to be their act and deed.

The whole case turned on what that document meant. Was it a deed that conveyed a fee simple title to the railroad, a release, or what? Edgar Bell was the senior real estate authority in the office, and he was consulted. After a careful reading, he said "I don't think we will know what that instrument is until the Supreme Court tells us." It was my good luck to be assigned to research the Pennsylvania law on this, and get the case ready for trial.

There were a lot of railroad cases decided by the Pennsylvania courts during the previous hundred years, and I set about reading them. Several legal principles quickly became clear: (1) if the railroad acquired its title by "eminent domain", it didn't get title to the underlying minerals, including the natural gas; (2) all the railroad had to do to get title by the right of eminent domain was to survey a proposed route and by corporate resolution approve and adopt that route for its railroad, and then pay damages to the affected landowners; (3) if the railroad got title by eminent domain, it lost that title when it ceased to use the right-of-way for a railroad, which then reverted to the then owner of the land on which it was located.

After a few weeks of reading the cases, and rereading every word of the document daily, I went to Mr. Eckert and said I suspected that the railroad had already acquired title to the right-of-way by eminent domain, and that their title was conditioned only on paying damages to the landowners. If this was the case, it explained what the purpose of the document was: to get a release of damages, not to convey a fee simple title. Could we get the corporate minutes of the S & S railroad for 1903 and before? No problem, he said, we will subpoena them, which we did. Soon I was on my way to Baltimore, armed with my subpoena, to examine the minute books of the S & S, now in the corporate offices of the B & O Railroad.

I was more than a little excited by this prospect and, to my delight, there I found the corporate minutes adopting the surveyed route several months before the date of our instrument. I returned to Pittsburgh (on the B & O Railroad, of course) with the happy announcement to all that we were going to win this case. I was now convinced that the railroad had acquired its rights by eminent domain, and that this was the release of damages that was the final step in that process.

Everything fit neatly into that interpretation, except for one little nagging fact. The instrument described the strip of land as four rods in width, which is sixty-six feet. Under the railroad statute, the railroad could only acquire a sixty-foot right-of-way, except where there were cuts and fills. Zeke and I drove up to inspect the property, and yes, the railroad had been built on a fill, and was about ten feet higher than the surrounding land. Maybe that could explain away the extra six feet. There was one little problem with that theory: the document said four rods in width, "and, through cuts and fills such additional widths as may be needed for slopes". These words were in the printed part of the form, but had been exxed out before it was recorded.

Well, so the theory wasn't flawless. I hoped that counsel for the defendants wouldn't notice this flaw. Our argument had to be that this was built on a fill, and therefore the railroad could take more than sixty feet. I was put to work on the trial brief.

The day for the trial came and it coincided with the first day of deer-hunting season. Rooms were hard to find in Emporium, the county seat of Cameron County, but we got a couple in a relic of a hotel. There wasn't much to the trial, as there weren't any disputed facts. We put Mr. Brookbank on the stand, to relate the facts to the court, and establish his title. He was deaf as a post, and the courtroom was cavernous with great acoustics, provided you were looking for a cathedral-like echo. He couldn't hear any question. After much shouting, finally Zeke got very close to him and spoke quite softly so the echo wouldn't confuse him. We got through that. The instrument establishing the railroad's title was introduced, and we called a civil engineer to testify to the height of the fill that the tracks were built on, without giving any explanation of why we were doing this.

We filed our trial briefs (this was non-jury, before a judge who would determine the facts as well as the law), and advanced our theory that the railroad had already acquired title by eminent domain, and the instrument in question was the release of damages necessary to complete their title. We pointed out that it could acquire more than sixty feet where there were cuts and fills, and this was on a fill. Happily, the opponents did not see the small flaw in this argument, which was: why did the document provide for more than four rods where there were cuts and fills?

In due course the judge, Trambley, J., decided the case in our favor, completely agreeing with our theory of the case. Significantly, the judge found as a fact that the nature of the terrain required a strip more than sixty feet in width, thus justifying a taking of sixty-six feet. The defendants immediately appealed to the Pennsylvania Supreme Court, which in those days had jurisdiction. (Today the appeal would go to the Superior Court). I was delighted. Fresh out of law school, and I get to write a brief for the Pennsylvania Supreme Court in a most interesting case.

The defendants hired Reed, Smith, Shaw & McClay, Pittsburgh's then largest law firm, to represent them on appeal. A former judge, Elder Marshall, was to argue the case for them. Obviously, Bill Eckert for our side. The new lawyers saw that the weakness in our case was the four rods-sixty feet anomaly. However, they were faced with a finding of fact by the lower court that the nature of the terrain required more than sixty feet for the railroad. They took the position in their brief that there was no testimony to support this finding. I knew we had them: they either didn't know the record below, or made this argument out of desperation. In our reply brief, we showed the testimony of our engineer, and a photo of the elevated railroad bed. So that argument was shot down, and they lost the appeal. The decision (*Brookbank v Benedum-Trees Oil Co.*, 389 Pa.151 (1957)) wasn't unanimous, but there was only one dissent, Justice Musmanno, and he didn't write an opinion, so we don't know what he thought. It still cheers me to read the majority opinion, but I was a little sad when it was over. I thought I would never have another case as interesting as my first one.

I have since often wondered how that four-rod description got into that printed form. It was either a mistake, or, perhaps a better theory, it was copied from a form used in some state that permitted a sixty-six yard taking by a railroad. It remains a mystery

12

The Associate

You may have noticed that four years slipped by as the Brookbank case wended its way through the courts. There were a lot of other things happening during those years, and this chapter will recount some of those tales.

You will recall that Ginnie was pregnant, shortly after the bar exam, as it turned out, and she quit working at Christmas time, 1953. She decided that she would like to have Ced Dunn, her family's friend and doctor, deliver the baby. He practiced in Beaver Falls and New Brighton, and at the New Brighton hospital. She stayed at her parents' house the last few days, and I spent the weekend of April 25 there. Ced decided the baby was ready, and had Ginnie take a dose of castor oil on Sunday night to get things started. I didn't have much confidence in what sounded like a rather old-fashioned remedy, so I left to go back to our apartment that night in order to go to work on Monday morning.

Ginnie called Monday morning to say that her labor had started. I jumped into our car (it was the 1950 Packard bought from my father) and set a new speed record between Mt. Lebanon and New Brighton. I needn't have rushed, but we left shortly for the hospital. It was an unseasonably warm spring day. I was allowed to stay with her in the ward (they didn't have a labor room) through the morning, but I wasn't of much help. We hadn't had any training in this, as modern parents do, and neither of us had much of an idea of what to expect next. She continued to have labor pains but didn't seem to be making much progress through the morning. I went back to have lunch with Ethel, who tried to stay calm by doing her Monday morning wash, and then I reported back to the hospital.

The pains got worse, and I got more nervous and scared, and finally in late afternoon the nurses chased me out to the hallway, where I could do the expected paternal pacing and hand-wringing. I was greatly relieved to see Ced appear, who gave me a cheerful wave and proceeded to the delivery room. I suppose it was only a few minutes, but they were very long minutes, when he reappeared and asked, with a big grin, if I would like to see my new red-headed son.

I was allowed to go back in to see Ginnie and a little wrinkled boy who looked damn mad at having been disturbed. I was astounded, because when I had last seen her she was in great pain, and I was wondering if she would survive. Now she was smiling and happy and looked wonderful. What a transformation!

As you may have heard, we named him Thomas Edward. We had a girl's name picked out also, as this was long before the modern inventions that show the sex of the child very early. Born on April 26, 1954, what a happy day. But not all the days after were happy. He cried a lot, and was what we then called a "colicky" baby. Whether it was the formula, or having to give up breast feeding, we couldn't figure out. But like all babies, he eventually outgrew that about the time he got started on more solid foods.

Getting back to the practice of law, I should tell you a little about the men in the law firm, and yes, it was only men, as female lawyers were rather rare at the time. The senior partner was William Watson Smith, and he was a dignified, tall man in his late eighties. He was regarded with awe by all those who had practiced with him, and had a reputation as a leading trial lawyer of his day. He did little at this time, but came to the office regularly. After the firm split in 1958 (and I will get to that) I never saw him again.

John Buchanan was the next in age, being in his seventies. He was still practicing, and was a leading light in the American Law Institute. He had benefited from a classical education at Princeton and Harvard Law School (where he finished second after Robert A. Taft of Ohio), and continued to speak and write Greek and Latin all his life.[1] I became one of his favorite associates, and worked with him on several matters, including the estate of Janet McCune, who died around 1956. I

---

1.   His language erudition was well known. At a dinner meeting of the World Affairs Council, he was slated to introduce a Chinese diplomat. The person introducing Mr. Buchanan said, "He may even introduce him in Chinese." Hearing that, John arose and introduced the speaker in Greek. The audience cheered, thinking he was speaking Chinese. Only the diplomat was puzzled. A few days later, two FBI agents came to his office and asked for help in translating some document in Chinese.

was asked to read all the cases on a subject called "blockage", a concept in Federal estate tax law. The principle involved estates holding large blocks of stock that could not be readily marketed without disrupting the market price. If the block were that large, then the estate did not have to use the market price on the date of death in valuing the estate, but could take some discount from that price. There were about a hundred cases that I dutifully read and annotated. Since they were fact-specific to each case, only the most general principles could be gleaned, but one got some feel as to how to make such claims. The estate was large for that time, around $60 million, and there were several large blocks of stock in her estate for which we claimed, and got, blockage discounts. The experience was important for me, because I got to know her sons, Charles and John McCune, and much of my later practice involved Charles McCune and his bank, The Union National Bank of Pittsburgh.

Frank Ingersoll was next in age, just a few years younger than John Buchanan. He had been a successful trial lawyer, and had tried much of the Alcoa antitrust case in the 1930's. He was a director of Armstrong Cork and Union National Bank, and it never occurred to me then that I might succeed him in those positions. He was a colorful and strong-willed personality. He could be rather irascible, and I did not always feel easy with him, but he could be kind and generous as well. When he was selling his large house in Fox Chapel, he gave their clothes dryer to Ginnie, and we used it for decades after that.

Paul Rodewald, father of my classmate, Bill, was the senior tax partner of the firm. He was a wonderful mentor to all the young lawyers, and his barnyard sense of humor, derived from his rural youth in Wisconsin, was a constant source of entertainment. He liked to hold forth at lunch at the Harvard-Yale-Princeton Club, which I soon joined. He was an experienced bird-watcher and naturalist, and Ginnie, Glenn and I accompanied him on a memorable wilderness canoeing trip to Canada in the 1960's.

Bill Eckert was about the same age as Paul, and was the firm's senior trial and appellate lawyer. I have already mentioned him in connection with the Brookbank case. His was a much more reserved and distant personality, not the extrovert one usually thinks of as a trial lawyer, but his thorough preparation of every case was a model for all lawyers.

Now that I have reached the ages of these giants of my youth, I think how fortunate I was to have been associated with them. They were all excellent lawyers, and each could teach a young lawyer a different set of skills. I think fondly of them and all the others: Bill and Emory Kyle, Elmer Meyers, Dave Buerger, Zeke Seamans. I had much to learn and they had much to teach.

But in every law firm, there are forces holding the firm together, and other forces pulling it apart. Human nature leads most lawyers to think that his accomplishments aren't fully appreciated, that he should perhaps be getting a larger share of the firm's profits, or that others may not be working as hard as he is. Given the assertive nature of lawyers, I marvel that many firms can survive for long periods of time. But in 1958, Glenn and I and the other associates were shocked to find that the firm had split. Bill Eckert, Zeke Seamans and Carl Cherin had decided they should take over the firm and retire Buchanan and Ingersoll, but the other partners would not go along. So they left the firm to start a new one. The new firm had Alcoa for a client, and the seceders believed others would follow. Mr. Smith said he felt sorry for them and would be "of counsel" to them.

Both firms wanted most of the associates to go with them, and we had a few anxious days in trying to sort this out. A lot of energy and vigor was going with Eckert, Seamans & Cherin, as their firm was named. We thought we would make more money at Eckert Seamans, and might have bargained for a partnership. But both Glenn and I did not feel quite right about their attempted coup, and in the end decided to stay with the old firm. Jim Park, Jim Morton and Jack Armstrong, other friends and associates of our age, made the same choice. But friends Mel Mellott and Gregg Kerr left. Looking back, I have no doubt that I made the right choice, and probably Mel and Gregg feel the same way.

So the firm now became known as Buchanan, Ingersoll, Rodewald, Kyle & Buerger, and the rest of my legal career was spent with that firm.

Meanwhile, back home, our lives moved on. We left our apartment on Shady Drive East, and moved into a double-home on Mabrick Avenue, which we shared with our good friends, Ted and Celeste Gallup. Tommy had turned into a cute redheaded boy of two when our first daughter, Barbara Lowe, was born on June 21, 1956. She was a petite little redhead, and our lives were full with our little family. It was a nice arrangement as we could share babysitting chores with the Gallups, and found that if we put the babies (they had two the same age as ours) near the fireplace, we could play bridge in one of the living rooms and hear a baby in the other if he or she cried.

We had joined Southminster Presbyterian Church (then Mt. Lebanon Presbyterian) when we came to Mt. Lebanon, and our children were baptized there. Tom was quite vocal when he was anointed, and we decided to wait until Barbara was a little older before presenting her for baptism. I joined the Chancel Choir of the church in 1956, and continued to sing tenor there for more than forty years. When the children were grown, Ginnie joined as a soprano.

In 1957, we found that another baby was on the way, and so we needed more space and looked for a house we could buy. We found a small three-bedroom house in Mt. Lebanon at 928 North Meadowcroft, located on a hill, with woods behind it. We managed to come up with a $500 down payment, and borrowed the balance of $17,000 from Union National under a G.I. mortgage, with an interest rate of 4.5%. We drove down to look at it the night we had the closing, and it was a bright moonlight night and we were quite proud of our new home. It was our house, or, as I said at the time, ours and the bank's.

We had a rather dismal Christmas that year. Both Ginnie and I got sick with the flu a few days before the holiday, so Wib and Ethel came and took our two little kids home with them (Ginnie was expecting any day) and left us to our miseries. We were able to stagger around by Christmas day, so the Gallups invited us to dinner at Ted's parent's home. We weren't able to eat much, but were grateful for the distraction from feeling sorry for ourselves.

Our daughter Susan arrived three days later, and was our first child with dark hair and complexion, like her two grandmothers. We had despaired of her arriving before the first of the year, and thereby losing the income tax exemption for 1957. I had promised the tax refund to Ginnie for new clothes if the baby arrived on time, and Susan, showing her usual good legal judgment, did just that.

The 1950s were happy years: graduating from college and law school, getting married, getting a job, getting started in a career, beginning our family. I got to know many of the clients that would be important to my future: Armstrong Cork, Union National Bank, the Guttman family, the McCune family, and many others. Looking back, it seems that much of my future was begun in that period.

13

The New Partner

Before leaving the 1950s, I will mention one more case I became involved in that
was unique: it was the only criminal law case I ever worked on. In early 1957,
John Buchanan was appointed by the Court of Appeals for the Third Circuit (the
intermediate federal appellate court) to represent an indigent state prisoner who
had been released on a writ of habeas corpus by the Federal District Court. The
District Attorney of Allegheny County had appealed the lower court decision to
the Court of Appeals, and that Court thought that the prisoner should be represented, as a significant constitutional issue was raised by the appeal. John was just
about to leave for a holiday in Greece, and said he would accept the appointment
if the Court would name me as his co-counsel. They did, and when we received
the D.A.'s brief on appeal, Mr. Buchanan left me with the job of writing a reply
brief.

The facts of the case were as follows: James Woods, a young black man of about
my age, had been arrested and pleaded guilty to a series of armed robberies in
Pittsburgh. His *modus operandi* was to wait until a car stopped for a red light,
jump into the car, and rob the driver. He gave his victims the classic highway-
man's choice: "Your money or your life." He finally was caught and was indicted
in the state courts, where he pleaded guilty. The court had not appointed counsel
to represent him in that proceeding. He was sentenced to forty years in the state
penitentiary. After serving ten years of his sentence, he applied for a writ of
habeas corpus in the state courts, on the grounds that he had not been provided
counsel, in violation of his federal constitutional rights. He lost, and appealed to
the Pennsylvania Superior Court, but his appeal was denied because he did not
have $12 to pay the filing fee. He petitioned the Federal District Court for a writ
of habeas corpus, which agreed with his argument and he was released. It was
from this decision the D.A. appealed.

The constitutional law question was pretty straightforward. At the time he was sentenced, The U.S. Supreme Court had held that a state must appoint counsel to an indigent defendant in a capital case. As this didn't involve murder, Pennsylvania had not appointed counsel. Some years after he had been sentenced, the Supreme Court held that the same rule applied in any serious felony case. And in the *Uveges* case (335 U.S.437) the Court held that this rule applied retroactively to any person who had been denied counsel in such a case.

So what was the D.A. appealing about? While his office grumbled about applying a constitutional requirement retroactively, the substantial point they raised on appeal was that Mr. Woods hadn't exhausted his state remedies, which was a prerequisite to filing in the Federal court. While he had tried to appeal to the Superior Court, he was turned down because he didn't have the $12 filing fee. The D.A.'s office claimed in their brief that he could have petitioned *in forma pauperis* for the appeal, meaning that if he had explained to the Court he couldn't afford the $12, the Court would have allowed the appeal. Now this was a novel point: I couldn't find anything in the rules of Court, or in any case law, that allowed for such a procedure. How would I deal with this argument?

I went over to the office of the Clerk of the Superior Court and asked if they had any procedure in such a case where the appellant couldn't pay the 12 bucks. The answer was "No", and thank goodness, because they got scores of these habeas corpus cases, and this disposed of most of them. I got them to show me their docket in which they had disposed of scores of such attempted appeals on this ground. So I got copies of the docket, and attached them to our brief. In short, I told the Court that the D.A.'s office was just blowing smoke, there wasn't any such procedure.

I got in touch with my client, and he came in to my office so that I could explain what the argument would be about. I asked him if he had heard of the Uveges case, and he said "Sure, Uveges was my buddy, in the same cell block, and I figured if he could get out, I could." Thus are jail-house lawyers trained.

I filed the brief, and Mr. Buchanan came back to the office before the case came up for oral argument. I assumed that he would want to argue the case, but he said he liked the brief, and that I should argue the case. I was delighted to do so. So one fine spring day, we took the overnight train to Philadelphia and walked from the train station to the Courthouse. Mr. Buchanan walked four miles every day, so I found that I had to walk briskly despite the fact that my legs were much longer than his. On our walk, he asked: "Are you joyous going into battle?" After pondering his question, I allowed that I was. He said that was a good sign, and that this was attributable to my Scottish genes. I always thought of that thereafter when going into court and always went into battle with a smile.

The three-judge panel that heard our case had read the briefs, and gave the Assistant D.A. a pretty hard time about his argument. I kept my argument short, covering just the salient points, answered a few questions from the Court, and sat down before I could talk myself into trouble. Mr. Buchanan reported to his partners later that I had argued the case "to the Queen's taste", which I thought was a very nice old-fashioned compliment. The Court affirmed the Court below, and we had won. Our client remained free. My career as a criminal lawyer was short, but my record was perfect. Never lost a case.

As an epilogue, I should add that I saw the Assistant D.A. a few years later, and asked if he had ever heard from my client again. "Oh yes, he was convicted of a burglary a few months later." I told him I was sorry, but glad that the client had learned some new skills while in the slammer.

As the decade came to an end, I got a pleasant surprise one December day, when Mr. Buchanan called me into his office and advised me that the partners had voted to make Glenn and me partners in the firm beginning January 1, 1960.

14

The Kids

Life is what happens to you while you are planning something else, as is often said, and our family life kept growing as I was busy practicing law. Our three kids filled up our little house on North Meadowcroft, and they had a good place to play in the backyards and in the woods behind. But it wasn't all pleasant, as we had our share of sickness and other problems.

One April evening when I happened to be working at the office, I went to the H-Y-P Club to have some dinner, where I got a call from a neighbor telling me that Tommy had been hit by a car and that Ginnie had gone with him to St. Clair Hospital and had asked her to call me. She didn't know anything more about his condition. I got a cab and had a most anxious trip to the hospital, where I found that the worst of his injuries was a broken leg from which he would recover. It appeared that he heard the ice-cream truck ringing its bell on the street, and ran out onto the street where he ran in front of a car. What a feeling of relief to find he would be okay.

He had to be put in a body cast for several weeks, to keep him and the leg immobilized, so we installed a bed on the first floor in the living room, so that Ginnie wouldn't have to run up and down stairs throughout the day. He was a pretty brave and cheerful little guy, for a four-year old, and eventually as summer came and it got hotter in that cast, he could have it removed. I remember taking him to the doctor's office to have the cast cut off, and he was a bit scared when the doctor started cutting through it with an electric saw.

He couldn't walk at first, and was fearful of putting his weight on his leg, but that wore off fairly quickly and he was soon running and playing as of old. As a high school student he ran on the Mt. Lebanon track team, and his quartet in the mile relay won the state championship in his senior year, so the broken bone hasn't slowed him down much.

On April 12, 1961, our daughter Laura was born, and the house began to feel a little small for all six of us. So in the spring of 1963 we began to look for something larger, and happened on what would become our new home, about a half mile farther into Mt. Lebanon. It was at 293 Dixon Avenue, a quiet little street about two blocks long between North Meadowcroft and Overlook. Here we had four floors and four or five bedrooms and could spread out, which of course we did. There is a garage and basement at the ground, or partly below ground level, a first floor with living room, dining room and kitchen, and bedrooms and baths on the second floor. The third floor had been used by the original owners as an apartment for live-in help, so it had two rooms and a bath. Five bathrooms in all seemed like a considerable luxury, after our one bathroom first home.

It was a lot of work moving, and since we were nearby we decided we could do a lot of the smaller things, like books, ourselves. That was a mistake, as while books may be small, they get heavy pretty quickly when loaded in boxes. But we finally got moved, and after that exasperating day I said that I didn't want to move from this house until I was carried out in a box. So more than forty years later, as I write this in my third floor office, we are still here, minus the children and only time will tell whether my vow will hold true. (It didn't: we moved into a smaller condo in 2003).

We were more than a little proud of our growing brood. If you look at pictures of us at that time, you can see why. Our three daughters were pretty young ladies, and Tom was a good-looking boy. They were all lively, although the girls were a little less trying than Tom, and we had the certainty of most parents that they were well above average in intelligence. That kind of confidence leads to high expectations when school begins, and they didn't disappoint us most of the time.

What kind of parents were we? That's a little harder to answer. I remember telling the kids on many occasions that I hadn't ever been trained to be a father, and the only way I could learn was by experimenting on them. Most of the time, I felt inadequate to the task. I think we were fairly strict with them, at least more so than they are with our grandchildren, and I don't know whether that was right or not. I can only point to the results, and say that they managed to survive our inadequacies as parents.

We think we did one thing right. I had three or four weeks of vacation each summer, and we always took a trip with the kids. After some fairly local excursions, we began to branch out, and went to a lake in Michigan, then a couple of trips to Nags Head, then we tried a few camping trips in a tent, then as the kids got older, we decided to buy a Nimrod camper, a trailer with a pop-up tent. That broadened our horizons and when Laura was five years old we launched forth on our first cross-country trip. We had a three-seat Rambler station wagon, and pulled our Nimrod. We first went to St. Louis, and then on to Arkansas where we stopped in Fort Smith and visited the Randy Warner family. Randy, you may recall, was my fellow Republican on the Law Review, and then had a busy practice in Fort Smith. Then on through Oklahoma and Texas, with a day's excursion into Mexico. There we ran into a problem. Laura's next-door friends, the Milie girls had come down with chicken pox just before we left, and right on schedule, Laura broke out on the day we visited Juarez. We soldiered on through the summer heat of New Mexico and Arizona, with the poor little kid looking worse and worse. We camped on the South Rim of the Grand Canyon, and did the usual tourist things like taking a plane ride through the canyon. We didn't try a mule train trip down the canyon, as our troops were a bit small, with one on medical report, but we had some hikes, one part of the way into the canyon. I took lots of colored slides, which we still look at from time to time decades later.

We circled around the canyon and had a nice overnight stay in Zion National Park, and then on to Los Angeles, where we could recuperate at Willard and Florence's house in El Segundo. Willard was then an electronics engineer with Northrup, and we had a high old time with them and Brian and Alan, their two sons. When we arrived with our trailer like a pack of Okies, Willard rushed out to tell us if we hurried we could still apply for unemployment compensation that day.

We had a good visit with them, and than headed East for home, via Sacramento, where we stopped to get the front wheels re-aligned, as pulling the trailer was hard on the vehicle. We came over Donner Pass, and relived that episode, and wound our way through Nevada and finally to Yellowstone National Park, with the geysers, and mud pots, and bears, and floating down the Madison River on our backs. What a treat! Then we worked out way home across country, and planned to do it again some time.

Our travels the next summer took us to Maine and the Maritime Provinces, and we toured around the Breton Peninsula and the rest of Nova Scotia and Prince Edward Island. It was a great trip, and we decided our goal was to show our kids the United States and Canada, and after that we would see the rest of the world on our own, and they could do the same.

15

Practice in the 1960s

Most of what lawyers do doesn't make for great stories: drafting contracts, wills, trusts or whatever. The work may be interesting or routine, but it won't keep a reader's attention. Litigation is one exception, so if I end up telling more stories about cases in which I participated, even though I never considered myself a litigator (nor did anyone else) it's because cases in court are stories.

Early in the '60s, Union National Bank decided to start a Consumer Credit Department. Of course, they had for years loaned money to individuals to buy cars and for other purposes, but that was largely done at the branch level. That type of lending was becoming much more regulated, with numerous statutes at both the state and federal level, and the management decided they had better have a central department with someone who specialized in that kind of lending to supervise what they were doing. So they hired an experienced consumer-lending officer from Mellon Bank, Lester Kerr. Lester said the first thing he needed was a lawyer, and he preferred a young one with no consumer lending experience so he could train him his way. I was eminently qualified, knowing nothing about the subject, and was sent to learn.

It was a happy move on my part, because not only was Les a good teacher and a good client, he became a good friend. He arrived with a full dossier of all the forms Mellon used for these loans, and set me to drafting all the specialized notes and other forms used in such lending. It wasn't heavy work: Mellon had employed plenty of good lawyers to work on them over the years, they were well drawn, and about all I had to do was read the statutes involved, and redo the forms substituting Union National for Mellon. I did occasionally wonder what would happen if I slipped up and left Mellon's name in some note and the debtor was directed to pay them, but it never happened.

As the loan portfolio steadily increased in size, we got to the more interesting side of the business, namely, what happens when somebody doesn't pay back the money they borrowed. The bank had a collection department that took care of most of that, dunning debtors, repossessing cars and television sets and the like. But occasionally they needed a lawyer to take some legal action, like confessing judgment or bringing suit, and that was where I came in.

We had a couple of memorable cases of that nature. One involved two motels in Toledo, Ohio. Now what was a bank in Pittsburgh doing lending money in Toledo? Well, the Consumer Credit Department loaned money to various leasing companies who would lease property and equipment, and one of those companies was run by a Pittsburgh man named Ernie Nappi. He had leased equipment and furniture to the motel owner, and the bank had discounted that obligation. The motels didn't work out, and while we made a number of trips to Toledo to restructure the debt, in the end the only solution was bankruptcy. There isn't much value in used motel equipment, so the bank ended up with a substantial loss on that loan. Since the leasing company was secondarily liable on the leases, it went into bankruptcy. Mysteriously, Ernie Nappi disappeared and was never heard from again.

Another business failure that worked out more satisfactorily was a used-car dealer in Beaver Falls by the name of Ron Henry. The bank financed his inventory of used cars, and bought the installment paper when he sold a car. The financing of the inventory was under Article Nine of the Uniform Commercial Code, and a word about that is in order.

The Uniform Commercial Code (UCC) is a comprehensive code drafted by the American Law Institute. It provides the rules for most commercial transactions, such as sales, banking, loans and other matters. Much of the code expressed existing laws and practices in the United States, but Article Nine was an entirely new provision for securing debts. It replaced a hodge-podge of techniques used in various states and provided a simple method of securing a debt. The debtor gave the lender a "security interest" in the collateral, which security interest was "perfected" by filing a notice of it in a public office, putting the world on notice of the lender's interest. If a store owner or automobile dealer sold the inventory, the buyer took free of the security interest, i.e., the buyer wasn't bound by the security interest, but the creditor's security interest continued in the proceeds from the sale.

Pennsylvania was the first state to enact this law, just at the time I started to practice. The code was familiar to me, as we had studied it in law school, even before any state had adopted it. Eventually every state in the United States adopted the law, making it uniform throughout the country.

One winter day I got a call from Les Kerr, telling me that they had been checking the inventory of Mr. Henry, and had found that he had sold several cars without paying the bank the proceeds as he was required to do. This was a sure sign that he was in financial trouble, and we acted quickly. A judgment was entered against him for the amount he owed, and we took possession of his auto inventory. This was no small undertaking, as he had cars in lots in several Western Pennsylvania counties. With the help of Glenn and several other lawyers, we got the sheriff in each of those counties to take possession of the cars and then drivers from the bank took them to a field we had borrowed for the occasion. In all, we gathered up about 400 cars in a short period of time.

The depths of his financial difficulties soon became apparent. He owed money to many others, including one small bank, Reeves Bank located in Beaver Falls, which had also financed several cars. He had given them the automobile titles as collateral. This practice is called "double financing" and of course is illegal. That poor bank had never heard of the UCC, and thought they were protected since they held the titles. That bank started a state court receivership claiming that they were entitled to the cars they had financed. This was heard by a judge in Beaver County, Frank Reed, and of course we filed a brief pointing out that we had a perfected security interest in the inventory, of which these cars were a part, and were entitled to them under Article Nine of the UCC. Despite much wailing and gnashing of teeth by the other creditors, and particularly Reeves Bank, the judge promptly held in our favor. Thus was the new law brought to the attention of Beaver County.

So there we were with about 400 cars rusting away and depreciating in value every day. We decided to hold an auction and sell off the entire lot at whatever price we could get. We advertised the sale, hired an auctioneer and, just as the weather turned to spring, started our sale. We had a good turnout of people looking for a bargain, and at the beginning of each car sale, one of the bank officers would stand up and announce that we could convey a clear title. The cars were snapped up at good prices, and the bank walked away happy. Ron Henry was so impressed by the sale that he decided to go into the business of auctioning cars rather than selling them as a used car dealer.

Enough of the consumer credit business. It brought me closer to Charlie McCune, who was pleased by the prompt action on the cars, and was a diversion from my more staid Orphans Court practice of estate planning and administration.

I continued to do legal work for Armstrong Cork and found myself in a difficult spot one day. Frank Ingersoll had been on the board of that company for about thirty years. I received a call from Albert Sheaffer, the Secretary of the company, and head of the legal department, telling me I had better come down to Lancaster and talk to him about a problem with the firm.

It appeared that at a recent board meeting the president, Maurice Warnock, had advised the board that the company had retained a Washington law firm, Covington & Burling, to represent it in an on-going FTC investigation of its pricing of floor products. Frank lost his temper and berated the president for hiring another law firm without consulting the board. Needless to say, this did not please the management who felt they could hire any law firm they wished. Albert suggested it was time for Mr. Ingersoll to get off the board, and would I take that up with the law firm.

Being among the most junior of partners, I did not look forward to taking on this formidable trial lawyer and senior partner, but if I did nothing the firm's long relationship with this client would be in jeopardy. I called Bill Kyle, an experienced corporate lawyer and long-time friend of Frank, and outlined the dilemma. He was reluctant to get involved, as he knew Frank would resent him interfering with a client he felt was his. Bill had not done any work for Armstrong in many years, but he did know Jim Binns, the Executive VP and soon to be successor to Mr. Warnock. He went down to Lancaster and met with them and listened to their complaints about our aging senior partner. They wanted the firm to ask him to leave the board, and Bill told them we could ask, but he would probably not listen. After some further thought, Mr. Warner decided it was up to Armstrong to tell him it was time to retire, which they did, and appointed Bill Kyle to fill the vacancy as director.

As expected, Mr. Ingersoll hit the roof on being advised of this, and called me into his office for a dressing down for my part in this coup. He demanded to know who had called me from the company with this complaint, but I declined to identify Albert. I told him this would do no good, and he should retire with dignity. He didn't like the advice, and our relationship was rather strained thereafter. It was a sad case of a good man staying on the job too long, and it left me with the conviction that I would retire from any job I might have too early, rather than too late.

16

Other Lives: Music and Mental Health

The years go on, don't they. I find myself in my 40s and the century in the 1970s. But before we go there, let me digress to some other parts of my life which don't fit neatly into a chronological order.

Both are related to our church. We had joined Mt. Lebanon Presbyterian Church in 1953 when we moved to Mt. Lebanon. It became Southminster a few years later when the U.P.'s merged with the Presbyterians (the Mt. Lebanon U.P. had seniority over us). I remember that Bill and Thelma Forrester came to call on us to recommend that we join the church. John Calvin Reid was the Senior Pastor then, an eminent preacher, and our first impressions were favorable, even though the front of the sanctuary was torn up while a new pipe organ was being installed.

After a few years, I thought I might like to join the choir. They seemed to be pretty good, and I had enjoyed singing in high school, and in a church choir in Philadelphia when I was at Pennsylvania Military College. And if you happen to sing tenor, it isn't hard to get a tryout with any choir. Paul Brautigam was then conducting the choir, and Gladys Klaber was the organist. She had been with the church from its earliest days, and was a seasoned accompanist. I liked the choir, and they liked me, and after a few weeks I found the music not too difficult. As I said, tenors are usually welcome.

After a few years, the two of them urged me to try some solo parts. I was reluctant, as I didn't have the training to be a soloist. But finally I agreed to do an incidental solo at the beginning of a choral piece (*Springs in the Desert*) by Arthur Jennings, a mentor of Gladys who had helped design the Southminster organ. I remember the feeling of stage-fright I felt at that time. But I survived the experience and was urged to do more.

I doubt if my career as a soloist would have gone much further, but Paul retired and Gladys left to be the organist for another church. Franklin Watkins became our organist-director, and I don't recall doing any solo work while he was there. But I learned a lot about singing from both Paul and Franklin and I think my voice improved as we went along. I enjoyed the choral work, and we sang the classical repertoire of good church music.

After a few years, Franklin retired, and I happened to be Chairman of the Music Committee of the Session at the time. So we began a search for a new director. We wanted someone who was more than a church organist or even a choir director. In short, we wanted someone who would lead the church in all possible musical directions. After looking at a number of candidates and many resumes, I was dispatched to meet a young man then leading a choir in Bristol, Delaware. His name was Thomas Flynn and he and his wife, Jessica, were recent graduates of Westminster Choir College in Princeton.

I flew down to Delaware on a January weekend (it was a Super Bowl weekend I recall) and attended the church where he was conducting. He had a very small choir, and I wasn't too impressed with their quality. But I had lunch with the two of them, and was impressed with their qualifications and the enthusiasm for what they were doing. He had a vision for the role of music in a church setting that involved many people, not just a few devoted singers. After further background checks, we decided to hire him. It was a happy choice, and more than thirty years later, and several Senior Ministers later, Tom remained the Minister of Music at Southminster until 2002.

He was as good, or better, than we could have hoped. He led scores of young people into music through his handbell program. His Senior High teams have performed throughout Europe and North America, and on three or four occasions at the White House. He led choirs of all ages, conducted various opera, plays and musical performances, both instrumental and vocal.

One of his first steps with the adult Chancel Choir was to announce that he was available for individual singing lessons, regardless of past experience or talent. I was one of many who took advantage of this, and for the first time I had a real voice teacher trying to make me into a presentable tenor soloist. His lessons, accompanied by advice from his wife Jessie, a talented soprano who also sang with the Pittsburgh Opera, taught me more about singing than I had learned in decades of choir singing. When we would get to the subject of how to modify vowels when moving into the high ranges, Jessie was called in as the expert.

I can't say I became a soloist of operatic quality, or even close, but over the years I did sing the tenor solos in many oratorios (Handel's Messiah, Mendelsohn's Elijah, St. Paul and many others), cantatas, many requiems and some modern works by composers such as Carl Orff. What it gave to me was a genuine appreciation of all of those great works, and when I hear one of them being performed now it is like visiting an old friend. Tom even got me to sing in a Pittsburgh Opera performance of Aida, in the chorus of course, and that was a singular experience. Barbara Karp was the producer, and the soloists were experienced Metropolitan and New York City Opera performers. It was wonderful to be involved in the preparation, rehearsals, the costumes and listen to real opera singers from the wings. And it is fun to sing Verdi's triumphal march at fortissimo. I have many fond memories of those nights, but I won't test your patience with those.

To bring an end to this, after forty years of singing with the Chancel Choir, and having reached the age of seventy, I thought it best to retire. I don't like the sound of old tenors, and after a performance by our choir at the Bruton Parish Chapel at Williamsburg, Virginia, I concluded that this should be my swan song. I must confess I still like to sing and I still go back to sing with the choir at Christmas and special occasions, and have sung occasionally with the little choir at the Federated Church in Orleans, Massachusetts, in the past few years. But we are going too far into the future.

I had some other tasks as a member of Southminster. I served terms as a deacon, trustee and elder, and one term as Clerk of Session. I also had a term as a trustee of Pittsburgh Presbytery. I suppose my acme in Presbyterian life was when my friend, the reverend Janet Edwards, was moderator of the Presbytery, and she invited me to be a vice-moderator. One should attend a meeting of the Pittsburgh Presbytery to get the flavor of what it is like to be a Presbyterian. We tend to be a contentious lot, but that's our heritage.

What does this have to do with mental health? Well, a lot for mine as a singer, but that isn't what this next story is about. Our church had a men's group that visited Mayview State Hospital, a mental institution, at Bridgeville once or twice a month. Mostly they played sports or cards or any activity that suited the patients. I didn't think I could contribute much to a basketball game, but one night I went along with the boys and took my chess set. They sent me to the geriatric ward and the attendant there asked if anyone would be interested in playing chess. Yes, came back the report. An elderly patient who says he was the Pittsburgh chess champion. I smiled, and said I was General Patton.

Guess what. He had been the Pittsburgh chess champion, and seemed like a fairly normal person except for some ideas he had about solving the Lindbergh kidnapping case through the use of chess principles. He played one game carefully with me, and won, and the next game he finished me off quickly. He could see that I was a mere amateur, but he told me if I would come back he would teach me and improve my game. He said that I had good potential but just hadn't been playing people of good quality, a fact that I conveyed immediately to Paul Rodewald who had been teaching me the game.

Well, I did get back for a few more lessons, but, alas, he died before turning me into a respectable chess player. But I got to know a number of the men in the church whom I liked: Frank Jordan, Bill Forrester, Ed Brindle, Dick Collins, and Dick Stein were among them, and I am sorry to say all have gone to join the Church Triumphant, as we say in the Presbyterian church. I miss all of them. Ed Sell, the long-time teacher of the Men's Bible Class was one of us, and also then the Dean of Pitt Law School, and was one of the few surviving members of the group (until 2004).

Bill Forrester, who had first urged us to join the church, suggested that I go to a meeting of the board of United Mental Health, a United Way agency in Pittsburgh. I did, and was persuaded to join the board. I spent a couple of years attending their monthly meetings and found their advocacy efforts interesting. Bill had been actively involved in the mid-sixties in getting Pennsylvania to change its mental health laws.

One day I got a call from Judge Malcolm Hay, an Allegheny County Orphans Court judge, and a member of the UMH board. He said he would like to nominate me to be the Vice-President of the board. I protested that I was busy practicing law, too inexperienced, etc. He fixed me with a stern look and said *he* had found the time to be president, besides I would have a couple of years to observe the about-to-be elected new president, George Day, an Alcoa executive. Well, all right, I would try it, and after all, I did have to appear before the judge on many occasions.

About two months after we had been elected, I got a call from George telling me Alcoa had just transferred him to San Francisco. Sorry, but I would have to take over for him. Shortly after that the Executive Director of the agency told me he was leaving. He and the agency hadn't been getting along very well with the United Way, and he thought his days were limited. I could only ask *"how could I get myself into such a pickle?"*

Life does take some strange turns. The first problem was to find someone to take the interim position of Executive Director while we conducted a search. None of the seven or eight staff people seemed qualified. Then someone suggested we approach a member of the board, Rosemary Plesset, to take on the job. She had been the Secretary of the Democratic Party in Pittsburgh when Dave Lawrence was Mayor and then Governor, was a protégé of Governor Lawrence, and was out of a job after he died of a heart attack. She had been trained as a psychiatric social worker and was married to a Pittsburgh psychiatrist. I had been impressed with her knowledge and energy as a board member.

So we asked Rosemary if she would mind taking on this job. She was a little reluctant, but since we promised it would only be for a few months at the outside, until we found a permanent replacement, she agreed. There are times when the Lord is with you, and the agency and I couldn't have been luckier. She took over quickly and decisively, and within a few weeks she had the agency performing more effectively than it ever had before.

She marched me up to the United Way to plead for a chance to show what we could do, and they agreed to continue our funding but let it be known we were on probation. After continuing our executive search for a few months, she confessed that she liked the job and would like to be considered as the next Executive Director. We hadn't found anyone nearly as good, and we gave her the job quickly before she could reconsider.

UMH underwent a burst of activity under Rosemary's direction. A typical performance was during Mental Health Week one spring. She called her old friend, Hubert Humphrey, then Vice-President of the United States, and asked him to come to Pittsburgh to speak at a mental health luncheon. She assured him that all the labor unions would turn out, as well as local politicians, and he promptly agreed. We had a great day with HHH, as he toured a handicapped children's hospital, spoke at our luncheon at the Hilton before an audience of 2,000, and appeared at an afternoon reception. I have a photograph somewhere of Malcolm Hay, Hubert Humphrey and me, smiling like the cat that swallowed the birdie.

I got to know John and Shirley MacIver through the UMH board. John was the house psychiatrist for U.S.Steel, and Shirley was practicing medicine at St. Francis Hospital. Shirley had retained her Cape Cod accent, and we teased her about introducing Hubert. She did well in the introduction in concealing her accent, until she mentioned the trouble in "parking" her "car" which come out pure New England, to everyone's amusement. We also invited Dick Thornburgh, then the U.S. Attorney for Western Pennsylvania, to speak at the lunch, thereby making it bipartisan. It didn't hurt Dick's career, as he went on to become Governor of Pennsylvania, Attorney General of the U.S., and to hold other high offices. I have been proud to call him a friend.

Rosemary marched me off to various meetings of Pennsylvania Mental Health and National Mental Health. She also once palmed me off as a "mental health expert" (she was shameless) on a television broadcast from Washington, D.C. Well, I finally finished my term of office, and absolutely refused to become President of Pennsylvania Mental Health (I still had to make a living practicing law). A few years later, however, the Allegheny County Commissioners appointed me to the County Mental Health/Mental Retardation Board, and I spent several years on that board, finally becoming chair for two or three years. In that job I had the pleasure of working with Chuck Peters, who was the best administrator in the entire state. The staff there supervised the providing of services to those populations, disbursing about $200 million of public funds annually.

One of the problems of the County program at that time was the lack of an agency to buy, hold and lease real estate to the agencies providing residences for the influx of people being discharged from state hospitals for the mentally ill and the retarded. The service provider agencies didn't have the capital or experience to do that, and we felt that a non-profit corporation could do that job effectively. Chuck kept bringing up this problem with me, and I kept saying that he should get the County Commissioners to give us some money and we would set up such an entity. It took a few years, but one day in the mid-1980s he came to see me and said he had the Commissioners talked into a grant of $1 million dollars to get us started in that enterprise.

So I incorporated a company that we named Residential Resources, Inc. We formed a board of directors and went to work. The first thing we had to do was to hire a CEO, and we were fortunate to find an enterprising young man by the name of Jerry Selia, who could wield a hammer, operate a computer and knew the mental health community. He had been operating a business of his own, and had all the job skills one could have wished.

It didn't take too much thinking to see that $1 million wasn't going to buy a lot of real estate, certainly not the scores of homes we were expected to provide. So we got the County to summon the four major banks to discuss this problem. I told them we would deposit the money in those banks (in certificates of deposit), and use that money as collateral for loans they should make for us to buy properties. They would also hold a first mortgage and we would assign the leases as collateral. And, by the way, we would like them to lend 100% of the purchase price, plus any improvements. I earnestly assured them it would certainly look good on the Community Reinvestment Act reports kept by the national banking authorities.

Union National Bank had already signed on (I was then the chairman of its holding company, but we will get to that), and Mellon and PNC soon joined after some pondering. We eventually made our first purchase of a normal residential home, housing four retarded persons recently discharged from a state institution. We were on our way, and none too soon. The county was inundated with patients being discharged from mental hospitals and state institutions for the retarded. I will abbreviate this tale by saying that in the years since that beginning, the corporation now owns more than $36 million of real estate, providing housing for more than 800 people who might otherwise be homeless. I wish all of my efforts could have been this successful and satisfying.

One story that combines these two elements of my life, mental health and singing, occurred in the 1970s. I was singing the role of Casper in "Amahl and the Night Visitors" at our church. It was conducted by Tom Flynn, of course, and Howard Douds and my partner Bob Johnson were the other two Wise Men. Jessie Flynn was Amahl's mother, and little Jim Tinnemeyer was the eponymous boy soprano. We had elegant costumes, and I was covered with a white beard and wig. I happened to be on the board of South Hills Child Guidance Center (an agency of the county MH/MR system) at the time and they were having a Christmas party the same evening after one of our performances. After the performance, Ginnie drove me to the party in full stage regalia. The guests were pleased to have a visit from one of the Wise Men, but they couldn't tell who it was under that beard. We had everybody guessing until I finally pulled off the beard to the amusement of all. One lady wanted to know what I was doing in the costume, and I replied that I had been singing in "Amahl". She wanted to know if it was the South Hills Village Mall, and was somewhat embarrassed when I told her it was Gian-Carlo Menotti's opera.

This is a long enough deviation from the chronological, let's get back to a proper place in time.

17

Practice In The 1970s

As I look through my old office diaries, I find myself awash in a sea of memories of people and of interesting cases. To keep this memoir in readable perspective, we must pass over most of these, but a few are worth noting.

Somewhere around this time, I had a call from Don Patton (no relation) the head of the Trust Department at Union National. They had a small problem with the Estate of Frank McCune, an uncle of Charles McCune. He had left a bequest of "1000 shares of Standard of New Jersey" to a charity. He owned 1000 shares when he signed the will. After he signed the will and before he died, the 1000 shares had been split into 4000 shares. In the audit of his estate tax return, the IRS wanted to allow a charitable deduction for the value of only 1000 shares. The family wanted the charity to get the 4000 shares, as they thought that's what Uncle Frank would have wanted. The only thing that would convince the IRS to allow the deduction was to litigate the question in Orphans' Court, and Don wanted me to bring this proceeding on behalf of the family who would have gotten the stock if the charity lost. What made it unique was that my client, the executor, and the family, wanted me to lose it!

I wasn't used to arguing a case that I was supposed to lose, which posed some ethical problems. I wasn't about to mislead the Court on Pennsylvania law, and I thought the legal issue of whether this was a "specific" or "general" bequest clearly favored the IRS interpretation. However, happily, I found a Pennsylvania Supreme Court case which raised the identical issue and which favored the opposite conclusion (the charity wins). After carefully reading the case and the prior law on the subject, I concluded the Supreme Court decision was wrong. But that was my salvation. I called the attention of the Orphans' Court judge to the Supreme Court opinion, and argued that it was wrong and should be ignored.

Telling a lower court to ignore a Supreme Court opinion is a sure way to lose, which we did, and the charity got the stock. I successfully lost the case.

What made the case memorable to me was that a few years later the Supreme Court had the same issue before it, and *mirable dictu,* overruled its earlier opinion on the ground that it had been decided incorrectly. Twice justified!

Two clients, Armstrong Cork and Union National Bank, became increasingly important in my practice, and I will describe the more important matters in which I was involved. For the Bank, I had some experience in bank acquisitions on various small banks, which were fairly routine involving only an application to the Comptroller of the Currency. But in 1969, a bigger opportunity arose.

Peoples Union Bank in McKeesport was the fifth largest bank in the county; Union National was fourth. Peoples Union had branches in different locations than Union National. Peoples Union was being pursued by a predatory group called the Parsons Group which was threatening a hostile takeover. We were the "White Knight" to save them from this threat, and a deal was struck. In accordance with standard operating procedure, Harold Gregg, the Secretary of the Bank, and I went to Washington, D.C. to pay a courtesy call on the Comptroller to discuss our proposed merger. We were greeted with a less than enthusiastic response. While the Comptroller has the authority to approve mergers of national banks, they are subject to review by the Justice Department for antitrust violations. The advice from the Comptroller was that Justice would certainly object to this merger under the antitrust laws and would probably sue to enjoin it. The Comptroller would be happy to see the merger go through, but we shouldn't proceed unless we were ready to fight the Justice Department in court.

The antitrust law on bank mergers was in a state of flux at that time (this particular merger would not pose any great problem today), and the Justice Department was riding high. We came back home rather discouraged, and immediately reported to Mr. McCune. Harold was ready to call the whole thing off, but after listening to our report, Mr. McCune said "Harold, would you have been willing to pay another dollar per share for this bank?" Harold said he would. Charlie said "Well, that's two million dollars and that will buy a lot of litigation. Let's do it." I was delighted.

Now all we had to do was to convince the Justice Department that they would have a fight on their hands if they tried to block the merger. In reading the bank antitrust cases, I had noticed an expert witness who seemed to carry great weight with Justice and with the courts. His name was Oscar Goodman, a professor at Roosevelt University in Chicago. He had testified for the Government in the landmark *Philadelphia Bank* case, and for the bank in a California case. In both cases, the trial judges relied heavily on his testimony.

I called the Professor, and described our proposed merger. He said "You'll never get away with it." I asked him if he would be willing to come to Pittsburgh to talk with us about it. He paused, and then said "Sure, I always like to talk to crazy people. My fee is $1,000 for the day." Done, I said, and a few days later he came to Pittsburgh and sat down with us at the bank and listened to our story. I argued that while this was a larger merger than Justice had been approving, we would still be just the fourth largest bank, but we would be bigger and better able to compete against the big banks. We had been a competitive thorn in their side by offering free checking accounts, and had finally forced Mellon and Pittsburgh National to begin free checking. In short, the merger would be pro-competitive.

By the end of the day, Oscar was intrigued. He agreed to be our expert, and to help write the brief on competition that had to be submitted with the application. What fun that was! We worked on that brief for six months and enjoyed the whole time. Oscar had a great sense of humor, and was ingenious in thinking up theories to confound Justice. He also had a prodigious appetite, and loved the Bank's cafeteria. Every lunch time, he would fill up two trays with food, eat it all, and marvel at how cheap the price was.

He visited all the branches of both banks, and came up with this theory: Allegheny County was so geographically subdivided by rivers and hills that it could be divided into seven different submarkets. When one did this, then it was clear that Peoples Union and Union National were in entirely different submarkets. That and free checking were the two principal arguments of our elaborate brief, which was anything but brief. It was about the size of a Sears Roebuck catalog when we finished, about six months later, filled with maps and data and arguments. I did most of the writing, and Oscar did most of the thinking.

So, our brief and application were finally finished and sent off, and we sat back to see what would happen. It took several months to get an answer. The Comptroller approved the merger and sent it off to all the agencies, including Justice, for their comments. We knew what to look for in their response: if they said the merger would have an adverse effect on competition, that meant they wouldn't sue. If they said it would have a *substantial* adverse effect on competition, that meant they would sue. After weeks of anxious waiting, we got their letter: it would have an adverse effect on competition. We were home free.

There was much cheering, and I wondered around the office with a big smile. One of my partners asked me why I was so pleased. I told him that the Justice Department had said our merger would have an adverse effect on competition. He couldn't understand why that would make me happy; he just didn't understand the code.

A footnote about the Parsons Group: they had consulted Reed Smith's antitrust expert who had advised them to wait while our application was pending, because we didn't have a chance of getting the merger approved. The Group ultimately came to a bad end. Their practice was to buy banks for cash, which they borrowed from a large New York bank. Their strategy after buying a bank was to sell off its bond portfolio and invest in bonds of less than investment grade quality that had a higher yield, thereby increasing the bank's earnings. This was based on analysis by an economics professor who was part of the Group. The theory was fine until we had an economic recession, when the junk bonds defaulted and the lender had to foreclose on its loans, and the Group lost all their banks. So much for that investment theory.

In the course of that merger I got to know Jack Markovitz, the financial reporter for the Post-Gazette. He liked the story, and ran a number of articles that were pro-Union National and anti-Parsons Group. Some of them found their way into our brief. We talked many times later about bank stories, as he liked Union National and was fascinated with Charlie McCune.

I got to renew my acquaintance with Oscar Goodman a few years later. This was in connection with the *Miller* case, the most complex and interesting bank case I was ever involved in. It involved a rather ingenious embezzlement by one John Miller. He was an auditor for a company called West Penn Administration, which handled pension funds for several construction unions. Contractor-employers were required to pay amounts determined by union contracts for each union employee working for them. The checks were made payable to Pittsburgh

National Bank, which had a depository arrangement with each of the unions. The checks were made payable to "Pittsburgh National Bank" followed by the name of the union account, for example "Carpenters Account".

The checks were sent by the employers along with a form showing the names of the union employees, the number of hours worked, etc. West Penn would then deliver the checks to PNB for deposit. John Miller, one of West Penn's internal auditors, discovered how easy it was to intercept the money. He would open the returns, take out the check, and enter into West Penn's computer that the return had been received "without payment". Subsequently he would go back into the computer file and erase the "without payment" notation.

So now he had the check, what could he do with it? He had a moonlighting job working for one of the contractors, and had access to that company's checking account. He took two or three of these stolen checks, typed an endorsement on the back that corresponded with the payee described, for example "Pittsburgh National Bank-Carpenters Account" and endorsed it over to the account of his moonlight employer "for deposit only". He took a few of the embezzled checks down to the branch office of Union National, which happened to be located in the same building as West Penn. He was known in that office as an auditor for West Penn, and he explained that these checks were improperly made out and should have been deposited to the account shown in his endorsement. It was a simple screw-up that could be corrected by transferring them to that account which was also in that branch.

The unsuspicious cashier accepted them for deposit to the latter account, stamped "prior endorsements guaranteed" and sent it in the ordinary course of business to the bank on which the embezzled check had been drawn. By coincidence, the first one was drawn on Pittsburgh National Bank. So PNB was the payee of the check and the payor bank, and Union National had guaranteed what purported to be PNB's own endorsement.

Are you still with me? So John now had the money in his contractor-employer's account. He kept the books for this small company, and also had blank checks that had been signed, at his request, by this employer. When the money arrived in that account, John used one of those blank checks to withdraw it and deposit it in his personal account. It worked: he was onto a good thing.

He kept this up for many months, eventually embezzling more than a hundred checks, for a total of $440,000. But one day one of the contractor's noticed this strange endorsement on one of their returned checks, and came to West Penn to ask for an explanation. John was called in to explain this anomaly, and he excused himself to get something from his office. He walked out the door, not even stopping to pick up his overcoat (it was winter) and disappeared. He had no wife or family, and he couldn't be found anywhere.

Union National soon heard about this. West Penn's lawyers arrived to demand that Union repay the $440,000. After all, we had guaranteed the endorsement which had been forged. I was called by an anxious bank officer to do something about this mess. With help from my partners, we quickly filed a writ of "Fraudulent Debtor's Attachment" with every bank in Pittsburgh and surrounding counties. This writ attached every account in the name of "John Miller" in each of these banks. That is a rather common name, and we would review each account under that name in each of the banks, and released most of them. Most were in joint names of husband and wife, and we could eliminate those quickly, because our John had no wife. One of the accounts I was concerned about was the account of John Miller, who was the Chief Judge of the Federal District Court in Pittsburgh. He was well known to me as he was the Chairman of the Board of Westminster College. We quickly released his account.

The quick action produced some results. John hadn't had the time to close his personal account, and we recovered more than $300,000. We offered that to West Penn in exchange for a release, but they refused and brought suit against Union National.

John, in the meantime, had fled to Texas, where he took a new name, got a new social security card, and landed a job as an accountant for a company in Dallas. After several months, when nobody came to arrest him, he came back to Pittsburgh and turned himself in to the FBI. We talked to him, and he was helpful in finding some more of the money, and we eventually got up to $390,000. When he was sentenced, I appeared in court and recommended leniency because of his cooperation. I also visited him in jail, as I wanted to have John on our side when we got to the litigation.

So what kind of defense does a bank have when they have guaranteed a forged endorsement? By then I had enough banking experience to know that this wasn't a lost cause. The Uniform Commercial Code, which we have already mentioned, provides a defense (§3-404) if West Penn and Pittsburgh National had been negligent in allowing this forgery to happen. There is a pattern in these cases: the employer of the embezzler thinks the bank is at fault for paying on a forged endorsement, and the bank thinks the employer is at fault for hiring the guy in the first place and letting him get away with it.

So we had to show that West Penn was negligent. That wasn't too difficult; their method of handling checks was so sloppy that anybody could pilfer them. We also had a favorable witness in John Miller, who hated the manager of his former employer. He was happy to point out how easy it was to steal from them. We also had the unusual circumstance that Pittsburgh National was one of the banks on which the checks were drawn. They got the check with their forged endorsement on it and paid it. This happened many times. We could argue that they were now precluded from denying the endorsement (lawyers call that "*estoppel*" which is a rather nice word, don't you think?). Union National had relied on the fact that PNB honored this endorsement.

There was one problem with our defense. Under §3-606 of the UCC, we had to show that Union National had acted in accordance with "reasonable business standards", whatever that means. We knew what their expert witnesses would say: no bank should ever accept a check payable to one corporation (PNB) and deposit it to the account of another corporation. I pondered this dilemma for some time. One morning while walking to work (I used to park near Station Square and walk across the Smithfield Bridge into town) an idea came to me. Nothing is more routine for a bank teller than to accept a check "for deposit only". He or she isn't passing out any money, the check is going into another account at that same bank, and if there is anything wrong with the check it will be returned by the payor bank. I thought any teller would do this. Why not test out this idea?

I talked to my partner, Clayton Sweeney, who was trying the case for Union National, who liked it immediately. We had Union National make out a check payable to "Union National Bank-Carpenters Account", typed the same endorsement on the back, and endorsed it over to one of our corporate clients "for deposit only". The obliging client presented it along with several other checks to a teller at Mellon Bank, who stamped the usual "prior endorsements guaranteed" and sent it off to Union National for payment, which of course, they did.

Now please notice that there was nothing fraudulent about this. Union National had authorized the check and the endorsement. The Mellon teller did just what I suspected any teller would do. (Our client, of course returned the money after it was collected). This was fun; why didn't we try it at some other banks. So we tried Equibank, with the same result, and then (holding our breath) decided to try it with PNB. Same result. Their teller accepted the check and sent it on. We were having so much fun, we tried it on the big banks in Philadelphia, with the same result every time. What all bank tellers do must establish what the "reasonable business standards" of the banking industry are.

Now we had only one last problem: how to get these checks into evidence. Clayton said "That's easy. We just get an expert witness to introduce them." Did I know any expert witness? Sure, let me call my old friend Oscar Goodman in Chicago. He knows everything about banking, and even wrote the article on banking for the Encyclopedia Britannica. Oscar was delighted to be of service. He would treat our experiment as a scientific and scholarly study by him to determine what the reasonable business standards of the banking industry were.

The trial was great fun. Clayton did all the heavy work, and I was just there as the UCC expert if one were needed. John Miller's testimony was devastating to West Penn on the negligence question. The manager of West Penn was a rather arrogant CPA who attempted to defend their practices. After three days of the best cross-examination I have ever heard (by Clayton), he was destroyed. It ended with him stammering and unable to answer any question. Their negligence was clearly established.

Now for the hard part: they presented two expert witnesses, one a senior officer of PNB and the other from Philadelphia National Bank. Both were expert in their field. Both testified that their training of their tellers would prevent any teller from ever accepting a check payable to one corporation for deposit in another corporation's account. They produced their office manuals prohibiting this. No bank would think of doing what our teller had done. Before the Philadelphia expert left the stand, Clayton asked him to identify a deposit slip from his bank. He didn't know what it was for, but we did: it was for the deposit we had run through his bank.

Finally, it was our turn, and the great Professor from Chicago was called to the witness stand. He described his scientific study designed to measure what banks actually do as distinguished from what they say they do. We introduced all the checks we had deposited, probably about twenty of them. They were admitted into evidence without any objection from the West Penn attorneys who were somewhat stunned and didn't immediately understand what we were doing. The trial adjourned for the day.

The next morning, West Penn's attorneys tried to get the judge to exclude the checks from evidence. The judge just smiled at them (he was enjoying the case) and reminded them that they had been admitted into evidence without objection and they were going to stay in evidence.

With all the expert testimony, and the dozens of references to the Uniform Commercial Code, the judge finally called both sides into his chambers and said that no jury was going to be able to decide this case. It was just too complicated. He recommended that the findings of fact be made by him instead of by the jury. Both parties agreed, and we were secretly delighted, as the Honorable Robert Duggan was an intelligent judge and did understand the case.

In due time, the Judge handed down his opinion which found in our favor on all counts: West Penn had been negligent, Union National had acted in accordance with the reasonable standards of the industry, and Pittsburgh National was estopped because it had honored its own endorsement. Of course, we did have to give back the $390,000 of the stolen money we had recovered.

West Penn appealed the decision to the Pennsylvania Superior Court. When it came up for argument, Clayton was hospitalized following an operation, and I got to argue the case before the Superior Court. They gave appellant's counsel (an old friend named Bela Karlovitz) a hard time, and I had an easy argument. The findings of fact in the lower court were all in our favor. As I was about to sit down, one of the Judges stopped me with a smile and said "This case must have been a lot of fun to try." I agreed.

If you find the case interesting, I recommend reading the Superior Court opinion which you will find at *West Penn Administration v Union National Bank*, 233 Pa. Super. 311 (1975). It was in our favor, of course. I later met a professor from the

West Coast who teaches Articles Three and Four of the UCC who told me he uses this case in his textbook because it was such a good tour of those Articles.

Enough, for the time, about Union National.

18

Family Matters

Lest I give the impression that the only thing going on in my life was my law practice, let me get caught up with what was happening with our family. Tom graduated from Mt. Lebanon High School in 1972, and headed off to Bucknell University. At the same time, his mother headed off to graduate school at Pitt. Ginnie had decided she should get a master's degree in special education just in case she should ever have to go back to work again. It was hard work, combined with having to take care of me and the other kids, but she graduated in 1974, at the same time that Barbara graduated from high school.

Barbara went to West Virginia Wesleyan College, where she had decided she would pursue a degree in their four-year nursing program. That left only me, Susan and Laura at home, so Ginnie took a job teaching a class of learning disabled children. Her employer was the Allegheny County Intermediate Unit, and her group of students ranged from 4th to 6th grade. She found it to be extremely hard work: every step forward in teaching a child was usually followed by a step backward in the following week. She worked every night and weekend preparing lesson plans, with little in the way of psychic rewards in seeing the students advance. After one year of this, she yielded to the pleas of her husband and children and quit the job. However, she did continue on as a substitute teacher in special education for a few more years.

Susan left for Mt. Holyoke College in 1975. Tuition payments for three college kids did keep us working, but we have never regretted any dollar spent on education. When I look at tuition for our grandchildren, I think we were lucky to have paid our dues in the 1970s. So in 1976 Tom graduated with a degree in accounting and came home to Pittsburgh to take the CPA exam and go to work for the accounting firm of Arthur Young. He had met a young woman from New Jersey at Bucknell, Nancy Henschel, and when she graduated the following year, they got engaged.

Barbara also met her future spouse while in college. Niels Kiewiet de Jonge was from Ben Avon. His father, Joost, was a citizen of Holland, but taught astronomy at Pitt. During World War II he had served in the Dutch Royal Air Force, and his tales of crossing the Pacific just before Pearl Harbor, narrowly escaping from the Japanese in Java, and finishing flight training in the US and combat missions over Europe are so exciting someone should make a movie of them.

The year of 1979 looms rather large in our memories. Susan graduated from Mt. Holyoke, and decided to go to law school. But before that, she got a Fullbright Scholarship for a year of study at the University of Bonn. She had been accepted at the University of Chicago Law School, but they were content to wait for another year. Barbara and Niels got married in July, at Southminster of course, with a wedding reception at Chartiers Country Club. Tom and Nancy got married in October in the Presbyterian Church in Ridgewood, New Jersey. The prenuptial dinner party happened to coincide with the day of Charles McCune's funeral, and I remember a very close call in catching the last plane to Newark in time for the dinner. That was the last time I would run to catch a plane.

So what was happening to little Laura? In 1979, she set off to college at West Virginia Wesleyan, following in her sister's footstep, with the view of becoming a social worker. She didn't meet her prospective spouse there, but while practicing her profession after graduating she met a young fellow named Chris Norton, but that's a later story.

In the following Spring we flew to Paris where we met Susan and had a nice tour of northern France, following in the footsteps of my Dad in WW I. Out to Brittany where his artillery company trained, and east to Verdun where he participated in the great American offensive. It is an awesome sight to see the scores of French, German and American cemeteries along the Meuse River, and to think of the thousands that were buried in the mud of the shelling with no grave. I can think of no better sight to contemplate the horrors of war. More than two million people died there.

One story worth mentioning: we eventually got to Bonn, where I went to a class with Susan. The lecture was in German, of course, so it didn't advance my learning very much. But one evening we were invited to the home of the couple who had taken Susan in for a home stay before she began her classes. They were a distinguished couple, both lawyers, and both working for the German State Department. Herr Doctor Wilhelm and Frau Doctor Barbara Hoeynck were their names. Susan said she would have to translate for us in his case, because she didn't think he could speak English. He greeted us in perfect English, with an American accent no less. Susan looked at him with astonishment, and he said "You didn't come here to learn to speak English". He had never said a single word to her in English in all the weeks she had known them. Privately, he told us that he had been with Helmut Schmidt in Washington, D.C., and had spent time in Vietnam as a liaison with the American army. He proudly said that Susan's German "was almost without accent". What a memorable evening we had with this wonderful couple and we are forever grateful for the care they gave to our daughter that year.

Oh, maybe that's enough about family for now, we will have more later. But one lesson from this Chapter: Family Matters!

19

Tragedies

Before moving on, I think we should deal with several deaths that occurred in this period. I had gone through my life without losing any close family members, and wondered if I had some kind of charmed life. Grandma Patton had died when she was 88, but that was expected. The years since the 1960s have not been so kind.

One night in May 1969, our phone rang. There is something ominous in a ringing phone at 3 am. It was my brother, Willard, with the shocking news that his son, Alan, had been killed. Evidently Alan and some teenage friends had been playing Russian Roulette on the steps of their school with a pistol of Willard's. Alan had shot himself in the head. At least that is what the other boys said, and the police believed them, although Florence didn't. Willard did not want to break the news to our parents on the phone, and asked me to go to tell them in person in the morning.

We waited until morning to break the news to our kids, who were as shocked as we were. After they had gone to school, Ginnie and I set off for New Castle. I dreaded the task, and about half way there it dawned on me that it was my mother's birthday, May 16. She would think we were coming to bring birthday greetings. Some greetings. It was all I could do to keep the car on the road. When we arrived, she was running the vacuum, but put it away with happy smiles that we had remembered her birthday. I asked her and Dad to come into the living room, as I had some bad news to tell them. I never had such difficulty in forcing words out of my mouth. They were in their 70's, about the age I am now, and had been close to Brian and Alan when they were little. They were shocked as well, and I could only tell them what little I knew. Dad wanted to know if the pistol was his 38 caliber which he had given to Willard. It wasn't, but I didn't know that and couldn't answer his question at that time.

They called their minister who came to the house and tried to comfort them. Gaylord had gotten the news, and we agreed that he would come to visit our parents and that I would fly to California to represent the family at Alan's funeral. I flew out that afternoon, but what can one do or say to a grieving family that is of any help? Just being there was all I could contribute but I stayed for a few days until after the funeral. I wrote a detailed account of my visit for my parents, which Ginnie still has in her collection. I can't write about it even thirty years later without tears.

Willard was never quite the same after that. The feelings of guilt and grief never were far away. He did not spend the rest of his life in depression, and when he was with other people he seemed happy, but when alone with Florence his somber mood would return. Florence not only had her own grief to deal with, but had to deal with Willard's moods. In our family, it is agreed that Florence should be nominated for sainthood.

But life goes on, and part of it is dealing with the death of people near and dear to us. Ginnie's father retired from J & L Steel that summer, and he and Ethel headed off on a cross-country automobile trip. They got as far as Arizona, where Wib suffered a heart attack. After a few days in hospital, Ethel drove him home, where we hoped he would recover. But in November, early one morning he had another heart attack and this one was fatal.

Ginnie stayed with her mother until after the funeral. The day of the funeral we had an early snowstorm that made driving difficult and I hadn't got my snow tires on, and neither had anybody else. I went from garage to garage pleading for early attention, and finally found someone who would help, and we made it on time. At age 65, his death seemed premature, and we laid the blame on cigarette smoking, to which he had been addicted for many years.

Ginnie's mother, Ethel, stayed in her own home for a few years, but finally found that to be a burden, and moved into an apartment at Asbury Heights in Mt. Lebanon, near us. She lived happily there for many years until stricken with cancer at the age of 90. We still miss her.

20

Armstrong Cork

As I have mentioned, from my early days as an Associate I had done work for Armstrong Cork Company, a Pennsylvania corporation with its headquarters in Lancaster, Pa. The company had been a client of the firm since the 19th Century, when it had its origins in Pittsburgh. Thomas Armstrong, the founder, had operated a cork bottle-stopper business in the Strip District for many years. Shortly after World War I, the company expanded its business to make linoleum, and built its first plant for that purpose in Lancaster. Within a few years, that had become the main business of the company and the headquarters moved to Lancaster.

When I came on the scene, the principal businesses of Armstrong were the flooring business, which had changed from linoleum to vinyl flooring, both tile and sheet goods; ceilings, both wood fiber and mineral fiber tiles; and specialty industrial products such as pipe insulation, gaskets, and textile manufacturing products. But it was always looking for new business opportunities, and it expanded into carpets, when it bought E & B Carpet in Dallas, and furniture, when it acquired Thomasville Furniture in North Carolina. It also disposed of one business, two glass plants in New Jersey, which made glass bottles. Armstrong was a small factor in that business, and it couldn't compete with the giants like Owens-Illinois.

I had the pleasure of working on those acquisitions with Bill Kyle and Ed Schoyer, and my early merger and acquisition experience stemmed largely from those transactions. In the course of that work, I got to know the management personally and many of the directors. I am sorry that I never met the legendary Henning Prentiss, who had run the company for decades, but he retired shortly after I started in practice. I am happy to say that I came to know all the presidents succeeding Mr. Prentiss, and had a high regard for all of them and their business

experiences. Cliff Backstrand was the first of this line, followed by Maurice Warnock (universally known as "Moose") and Jim Binns, with whom I had worked
on the sale of the glass plants.

There are many happy memories of those days, but I can't relate all of them lest
this memoir become too many volumes. I do remember certain red-letter days
that stand out, such as the trip I made to Dallas with Bill Kyle and Charlie
McCune (who had been a director since 1930) when they were acquiring E & B
Carpet. They were attending a directors meeting and a tour of the E & B plant,
and I was there to try to get the SEC to approve the proxy material for the
merger. The SEC had raised a number of issues concerning greater financial dis-
closure to which the Company objected. In a lengthy phone conversation with
the Washington office of the SEC I got the examiner to back off their demands. I
was invited to the director's cocktail party that night, and was treated as a hero
for having prevailed over the SEC. It was a modest success, but the timing was
important.

I had a strange conversation with Mr. McCune in the Dallas airport on the way
home. He had just passed his 72nd birthday, and had served on the Armstrong
Board for more than thirty years. He told me that Armstrong should have some
age limit on how long one could serve, and he expected me to do something
about it. Me? I was just a lawyer; if I had made such a suggestion to management
they would have suggested I mind my own business. However, I remembered the
instruction.

Another special occasion followed the sale of the glass plants. There was some
complicated formula for further deferred payment if the buyer achieved certain
sales objectives (I always hated such agreements as they inevitably lead to dis-
putes). I looked at the proposed pay-out, re-read the contract, and after some cal-
culating concluded we were entitled to more shares of the buyer than was being
proposed. I called Jim Binns and told him that, and he thought I was rather pre-
sumptuous. Both their in-house lawyers and their investment bankers had agreed
to the buyer's calculation. Who was I to suggest they had made a mistake? Especially those geniuses, the investment bankers. I calmed him down and went
through the reasoning and calculations with him. He called back the next day
and said, "My God, you're right and the rest of those guys blew it!" Little things
like that do help a fella's reputation.

Well, the ultimate red-letter day happened in 1976. Bill Kyle had decided that it was time to retire from the board of directors of Armstrong. He had retired somewhat earlier from the firm, despite my advice that he was making a mistake and would never be happy playing golf at Hilton Head. He liked to remind me, after he had retired, how wrong I had been. On the r.l. day aforementioned, Jim Binns called and asked if I would be willing to go on their board as Bill's successor. I took not more than five seconds to collect myself and say "yes". He said "I thought you would", and I was duly appointed to the board at the next meeting. I was invited into the meeting at the end and was warmly greeted by all. The most significant event of that day was that it was the last day for Moose Warnock as Chairman, as he was succeeded by Jim Binns. So Moose and I could always say we had served on the board together, even if it was only for a few minutes.

I got to know a lot of remarkable people on that board, and I will tell you a little about a few of them. But that must wait, as we must get back to the other things going on in my life. But at the time I felt that this was a turning point in my life, and looking back that thought is confirmed.

21

Law Firm Management

Let's go back a bit, as I was involved in law firm management from the mid 1960's until the early 1980's. My initial interest perhaps stemmed from the firm split in 1958, when Eckert, Seamans & Cherin was formed. It isn't hard to see why law firms split up: the answer is usually money. Either the firm isn't making enough of it, or some partners think they aren't getting a fair share of it. It is more interesting to think what keeps firms together, and that is a more complicated thought process.

After a few years as a young partner, I believed that the firm could and should be run more efficiently but I wasn't sure where to start. I persuaded the firm to send me to a law firm management seminar in Philadelphia so that I could see what the experts were thinking and what other law firms were doing. I don't remember what I learned, but I did come back with the strong impression that most firms were no better than we were at the art of management. For example, I found that almost no firms prepared an income and expense budget for the following year. At least we had an expense budget, which was reasonably accurate, but nobody had ever attempted an income budget, on the theory that revenue was unpredictable.

Glenn and I talked about this and decided to try to prepare a budget for the next year. Instead of planning what clients would bring in which business, we focused on the lawyers. We divided the firm into five age groups, and reviewed the number of hours each group had billed the previous year. Then we multiplied that by the average hourly rate we believed they would charge. Adding this up gave us the expected revenue for the coming year, and with our expense budget, a complete budget of revenue and expenses. It was a nice experiment, but it would take a year to see how close we would come. Would you believe it, the actual billings came within one percent of the budgeted amount!

Having demonstrated the possibility of predicting income, we now had a useful tool for increasing net income. The firm could either increase the total number of billable hours or the charge per hour, or both. So the next year the firm adopted goals for the hours of each group, and the billing rates, and increased both. It is not too hard to guess what happened: a substantial increase in net income. I became a firm believer in planning.

The firm continued to grow, and it became unworkable to transact all the business at a monthly partnership meeting. I authored a memo suggesting that we elect a committee of five to meet weekly (we had breakfasts at the Duquesne Club), and that group was to select one of its members to be the managing partner to handle the day-to-day administrative matters. Glenn volunteered to be the first managing partner and was so elected by the firm. The committee was named the Operating Committee, which I thought was a suitably neutral term, and it was to report to the partnership at the regular monthly meeting.

The next problem to be addressed was how net profits were to be divided among the partners. That had been done by the three active senior partners, Rodewald, Kyle and Buerger. This was not going to work long-term. Other partners felt excluded from the process and younger partners would quickly become alienated. So, after ruminating about this, I wrote another memo proposing that we create another committee, which I named the Advisory Committee. Again, the partners were divided into five equal age classes (the total number of partners divided by five would be the number in each class). Then the firm would elect one member from each class, and this committee was charged with proposing a new schedule of income distribution each year. One member would rotate off the committee each year, and another person elected to represent his age class. The committee would then present its recommendations to the firm to be approved by the partners at the proper meeting.

Ed Schoyer later dubbed the memos proposing the Operating and Advisory Committees to be the "Constitution of the Firm", and when I retired I was pleased to be given a plaque saluting me as the "Father of the Constitution".

I served on the Operating Committee for several years. Ed Schoyer succeeded Glenn as the Managing Partner and held that job for several years, and when Ed got weary, I served as Managing Partner for two or three years before leaving the firm. I confess I enjoyed tinkering with these mechanisms and proposed several additional changes, which finally were adopted. The first was to hold an annual retreat at some place remote from the office, in order to consider more long-term strategies and also to provide some social interaction among the partners. We were growing rapidly, and the opportunities to talk to other partners and understand what they were doing were limited. The retreats helped.

Another, and even more controversial proposal, was that the Advisory Committee should hold a peer review of each partner annually. We had always done that with great diligence for associates, but once a person became a partner he ceased to be accountable to anyone. The committee was charged with meeting with each partner for about an hour to review with him (we still didn't have any female partners) what he had accomplished in the past year and what his goals were for the coming year. If anyone had complaints about a person's performance, this was the forum for discussing them.

I think this was one of my best ideas. I looked forward to my own peer review each year, because it was one of the few times you could get people to sit still and listen to you talk about yourself. And they had to listen! (You might guess that this is the kind of person that would write an autobiography.)

We had considered incorporating the firm for several years. The purpose was to permit the adoption of more generous pension and profit sharing plans than were allowed to a partnership. The issue was complex from a tax standpoint, and it caused uneasiness among all of us used to dealing with ourselves as a partnership. However, we took a deep breath and adopted the corporate form about 1979. Since I was then the Managing Partner, I became the first president of Buchanan Ingersoll Professional Corporation.

I thought my plate was rather full between the practice and firm management, but one day I got a call from John Murray, then the dean of Pitt Law School. He needed someone to teach Article Nine of the Uniform Commercial Code. I had once lectured with him on that subject, and his regular teacher had fallen ill. It was a final semester course for third-year students, and I decided this would probably my only chance to try my hand at teaching. So I agreed to teach a class at 8:00 am to 10:00 am on Monday mornings. It seemed to me that it snowed every Monday morning that winter, and the students, many of whom had already landed their job on graduation, were a rather sleepy lot. But I enjoyed the role of being a law professor, and I pointed out that I no longer needed to apologize for being absent minded, as that is what professors are supposed to be. Two of the students, Carl Cohen and Carl Rothenberger had accepted jobs at Buchanan Ingersoll, and I had to make sure they were absorbing all this learning It was nice getting to know the faculty. I already knew Ed Sell and Cy Fox and got to know a young professor named Mark Nordenberg, who went on to become the dean of the law school, and now is Chancellor of the entire University where he is doing a fine job. I should add that John Murray left to become the President of Duquesne University, and did a great job of moving that institution forward.

I conclude this chapter on a sad note. Glenn's health began to fail in the mid 70's. He was diagnosed with severe hypertension, and his pilot's license was suspended. He owned a small plane with another pilot and enjoyed flying. I took a couple of flights with him, one up to Canada to a remote fishing place and another around Pennsylvania. He decided to retire from the practice of law, and he bought a house for himself and his father in New Wilmington. His mother and sister had both died from cancer the previous year. One August night in 1975 I got another late phone call, this from Glenn's dad, Harry Reed. He had just returned from a trip to Chicago and had found Glenn on the floor of their house. He had died from a heart attack. I won't try to describe the shock and grief from losing Glenn, my oldest friend. The Allegheny County Bar has a custom of presenting a motion to adjourn the court on a given day in memory of a deceased member of the bar. I gave the eulogy for Glenn that day in court, and made the appropriate motion, with scores of lawyers and judges, all friends of Glenn, in attendance. I still miss him and have often wanted to tell him about things going on in my life.

22

Union National Corporation

Frank Ingersoll died in 1976, leaving a vacancy on the Union National Bank board of directors. George Kesel and Dick Edwards recommended me to fill that spot, and in due time I was appointed to the board of the bank. Charlie McCune was in ill health, and was unable to attend those board meetings, so I never had the experience of being on that board while he was presiding. Mr. McCune retained the title of Chairman, Dick was the Vice-Chairman and presided at board meetings, and George was the President and CEO of the bank.

It wasn't very heavy work. The board met once a month, in the newly created boardroom on the Mezzanine of the bank offices at Fourth and Wood. There was an Executive Committee, which more accurately might have been called a Loan Committee, which met in between board meetings and approved loans over a certain size, say $500 thousand, and a Trust Committee that likewise met and reviewed the operations of the Trust Department. Board members rotated between those two committees every six months. Each meeting began at 11 am and concluded at noon, when officers and directors adjourned to lunch at Room 1010 of the Duquesne Club, the bank's suite. The meetings made for a pleasant interlude in a busy workweek for me, and I enjoyed them.

I don't recall any substantial difference caused by my presence at these meetings, although I did lobby for and the board finally adopted an age limit of 72 for directors, as the board had become rather antiquated. When Harold Gregg was Secretary, he joked that his principal duties at board meetings were to help directors doff their coats and store their canes. But times they were achanging, and George, with his Executive V.P.'s, Bill Walker, John Echement and Dave Brubach were moving the bank out of its old habits and into more business-like behavior.

In 1977, the total assets on the bank's balance sheet for the first time exceeded $1 billion. The bank had been in existence for 120 years, and I remember thinking that it wouldn't take that long to pass the $2 billion mark. That milestone was passed only six years later.

In 1981 I did do something that made a difference. I had been following the efforts of the Pennsylvania Bankers Association to change the laws of Pennsylvania concerning bank branching. For years, a bank in this state could open branches only in the county where its main office was located, and any county that was contiguous to that county. Thus a Pittsburgh bank could only branch in Allegheny County and the four counties that abut it. Most bankers wanted to get rid of that 19th Century scheme, and the legislation being proposed would permit bank holding companies to acquire banks in Pennsylvania outside of their local areas, and eventually to branch throughout the state.

These ideas had been kicked around for several years, and I got the feeling that maybe the legislature was coming around to this view. The small banks outside of the big cities were adamantly opposed to change, as they feared that they would be swallowed up by the giants. (They were right.) In any event, one day I sat down and wrote a letter to Dick and George proposing that we form a bank holding company to own the bank. This would put us in a position to move expeditiously if the legislative change occurred. All the other major banks had formed bank holding companies years before in order for them to engage in the non-banking activities then permitted under federal and state laws, but we had never been interested in those non-banking activities and hadn't followed that path.

The time for that idea was ripe. The management thought about it, agreed and recommended it to the board of directors. The board approved the reorganization in July of 1981, and I started the legal work to accomplish that change. First, one set up a Pennsylvania corporation that would be the holding company, and got the permission of the Comptroller to create a new national bank, appropriately called a "phantom bank" because it had no powers. That bank was wholly owned by the holding company. The shareholders had to approve all of this, and did so at a special meeting in November of that year. In February of 1982 all the necessary approvals had been obtained, and The Union National Bank of Pittsburgh merged into the phantom bank, which changed its name to that of the old bank. The shareholders of the bank received the stock of Union National Corporation in exchange for their bank stock. I didn't know it at the time, but I had just created my next employer.

The change was timely. The legislature in 1982 did enact the banking law change described, permitting bank holding companies to own banks outside of their branching areas. We were now in position, along with all other bank holding companies, to expand. Nothing happened at first; the officers and directors of the corporation were the same as the principal officers of the original bank, and the directors the same. One would not have noticed any significant change in board meetings. The shareholders got certificates with a new name on it, and continued to receive dividends and stock splits as before.

By coincidence, I also represented a bank in Punxsutawney, Pennsylvania, called Keystone National Bank. How I came to represent this client is another story, but suffice it to say that I had represented the Doverspike brothers, Jim and Carl, and the Barletta brothers, Mike, Joe and Tom, who had taken control of the bank from another shareholder in a proxy contest in which I had represented them. I talked to them about whether they might be interested in joining Union National Corporation. A meeting was discreetly arranged between them and Dave Brubach and me, held aboard Carl Doverspike's yacht in Florida waters (who could spy on us there?). Our discussions continued that evening in a Boca Raton restaurant, where we assumed we would be unknown, but to our surprise one of our bank directors happened by and wanted to know what Dave and I were doing there. We told him we would explain later. So much for clandestine meetings.

The discussions were fruitful, and we eventually made a proposal to buy Keystone for cash, which proposal was accepted by its board of directors, and submitted to the shareholders for approval. It was duly approved, and after we had met all the regulatory requirements, Keystone was merged into Union National Corporation in February, 1983, less than a year after we had become a bank holding company. We were the first bank holding company in Pennsylvania to own two banks. Moreover, I had acquired a new pastime, buying banks, which I found quite interesting. Keystone added about $200 million to the total banking assets of the corporation.

Dave Brubach and I hit the road to talk to other small banks in Western Pennsylvania. Dave was an ideal person for this task; he had a quiet, unassuming style that inspired confidence in anyone listening to him. He had spent his career as an investment advisor perfecting that style, and I found it a joy to work with him. He was as comfortable as an old shoe. Eventually we met with Roy Buchman, the president of McDowell National Bank, located in Sharon, PA. That meeting led to discussions with the management and the board of the bank, and eventually to an agreement to merge that bank into Union National Corporation, the consideration being an exchange of Union National's stock for that of McDowell. That transaction, in due course, was approved by the shareholders of both institutions and by the Comptroller and others, and the merger was completed on September 1, 1983. We became the first bank holding company in Pennsylvania to own three banks.

That date was significant for me as well, for on that same day I left the practice of law and became the Chairman of Union National Corporation. How this came about represents one of the surprising turns that life can take. Let me start with the fact that I represented Kitty McCune Edwards, wife of Dick Edwards, and her brother, John R. McCune, IV. We will talk more about them in the next chapter. Kitty died from cancer in 1982, and Dick had taken a trip to Italy a few months later. When he returned in the spring of 1983, he advised the board of the bank (and the holding company) that he was retiring as chairman. He was ready to start a new life.

I never thought that Dick enjoyed banking, or the business world, but seemed to do it as a family obligation, and now he felt relieved of that duty. Surprisingly, George Kesel asked me if I would like to become Chairman. I declined; the bank could not afford to pay much, or at least it had not in the past, and I was making a decent income in the practice of law. This conversation took place in the summer of 1983. A week or so later I was talking to Ginnie about this decision and said I was sorry about it; it was something I would like to have done. I knew it would be an exciting time in banking with the changes in the law, and I thought that it was time for the holding company to become something different from Union National Bank. Also, after thirty years of practicing law, I was ready to do something else. Her practical advice was to forget the money and figure out some way to do what I really wanted to do.

I was then counsel to the McCune Foundation, created by Charles McCune, so I talked to the other members of the Distribution Committee, Dick Edwards and John McCune, about my being Chairman of the Corporation and continuing on as counsel to the Foundation. The Foundation was the largest shareholder of the Corporation, and I didn't see any conflict in the two positions. They both agreed, and when the Executive Committee of the Corporation met in August, I told them I would be interested in the Chairman's job. They were pleased, and at the next board meeting I was so elected. I parted company with my law firm reluctantly, not too surprisingly after a thirty-year practice, and sent a memo to the firm about the change. It was an awkward time, as Jim Park had just left the firm to become CEO of Union Electric Steel. Two of us leaving in a short period of time caused Jim Morton to send around a memo saying that, despite rumors, he was *not* leaving.

So, on September 1, 1983, I found myself as Chairman of the Board of Union National Corporation. My first day was not spent in the office, since it was the first day for McDowell Bank as part of Union National, and most of us spent the day in Sharon at the board meeting of that bank. My office, on the 21st floor of the Union National Bank Building at Fourth and Wood, was the large and fairly elegant office that Dick Edwards had occupied. It was the old boardroom of the bank, and had walnut paneling. George Kesel, Bill Walker and John Echement were on the same floor. Pat Drury, who had been my secretary and administrative assistant at Buchanan Ingersoll, agreed to come with me to the bank, for which I was grateful as we worked well together.

The first real challenge occurred just a few days after I had settled in. John Echement came to see me with the alarming news that a lending officer of the bank, recently fired, had written unauthorized letters of credit by the bank to support loans made by other financial institutions, including Westinghouse Credit and a Japanese bank. The potential liability was about $7 million. The borrower was a real estate developer who had induced the lending officer to write the phony letters of credit. My immediate advice was that we should not pay the letters of credit. The other financial institutions would have to sue us, which they did, resulting in several years of litigation. Everybody eventually got into the litigation: the bonding company for the dishonest employee, the directors and officers liability insurance company for the principal officers of the bank (they were sued for not having apprehended the crook), and of course the developer and the former bank officer. I had to keep explaining to George, Bill and John that there was nothing personal about the suit against them; we just needed to get their insurance company into the game. The litigation went on for several years, and was eventually settled with the bank paying about $2 million, mostly in lawyers' fees. The plaintiffs got only a fraction of their claims, mostly from the insurance companies. The only disappointment in the whole mess was that we could never get the U.S. Attorney to bring a criminal case against the bank officer. The F.B.I. had recommended that action, but the local office of the Justice Department didn't want to be bothered with such a complex litigation; they only wanted easy cases like bank robberies.

1985 was a big year for Union National Corporation. We decided to raise some capital in a public offering of convertible debentures. The issue was very well received, and we had offers to buy more than the $30,000,000 we were offering. George and I spent several days on the "road trip" to sell the issue, visiting institutional buyers in Pittsburgh, Cleveland, Philadelphia, Baltimore, New York and Boston. Since the debentures were convertible into common stock of the corporation, I recommended that the McCune Foundation buy $5,000,000 of the issue in order to protect its 20% holding. That decision became controversial a few years later in the Foundation litigation, but those objections were doomed.

We also were busy buying banks. Keystone bought a small neighbor, Citizens National Bank of Big Run. We signed a contract to acquire First National Bank & Trust Co., located in Washington, Pennsylvania. The principal shareholder of that bank was Louis Berkman, and through that transaction I got to know him and his son-in-law, Bob Paul, who became a member of the board of Union National Corporation. The Berkman family was a wealthy family owning Ampco-Pittsburgh Steel, and had recently acquired Union Electric Steel, the company of which Jim Park was the President. Bob was a good director and a shrewd investor, and has often advised me on investments in the years since we became friends. Finally, we acquired Valley National Bank, in Freeport, Pa. When these transactions were all completed, we had grown to $3.1 billion in assets.

The annual report for 1985 contains one other indication of the maturing of the corporation. When I became Chairman, the only officer of the corporation who was full time was me. The others were also officers of the bank. By 1985, George had left the bank to devote his time to the corporation, we had added a chief financial officer, Fred Gardner, and Rob Stevenson, our general counsel, was now more concerned with the corporation than the banks. A nice photo of the principal officers is contained in that annual report.

This may be a good time to consider the parallel life I was leading as counsel to and a member of the Distribution Committee of the McCune Foundation.

23

The McCune Foundation

I represented Charles L. McCune from the time Bill Kyle retired until the date of Mr. McCune's death in 1979. He was an interesting client, to say the least. He was the oldest son of a wealthy family (his maternal grandfather had been an associate of John D. Rockefeller, and the basis of the family fortune was stock in Standard Oil of New Jersey). His father had been the president of Union National Bank of Pittsburgh, which had been founded by Charles's paternal grandfather.

Charles was an indifferent student, and college had little appeal for him. He dropped out of Princeton and after spending a few years in the bank, left Pittsburgh to become a wildcatter in the oil patch of Texas and Oklahoma. He was good at it, and built up a successful oil company that he sold to Texaco for stock in that company. So he turned around and built up a second oil company, which he again sold to Texaco for stock. He once told me that "they have sold all my oil, but I still have their stock." That experience led him to prefer buying banks for cash, as the stock would remain out there forever. His two transactions left him as the largest individual shareholder of Texaco, and he served as a director of that company for many decades. His colorful life has been described in many newspaper articles, and in his own autobiography "Three Lives, and All of Them Mine."

I worked on several wills for him, the final one being in 1973. He had no wife or children, and his only relatives were his brothers, sister and the children of his younger brother John R. McCune III, who were Kitty Edwards and John R. McCune IV. Kitty was married to Dick Edwards and lived in Pittsburgh, but young John had an independent streak rather like his Uncle Charles, and left Pittsburgh to make a life on his own. He eventually became a state Senator for the State of Oklahoma. I also represented Kitty and John in their estate planning.

His will left a few million dollars to his niece and nephew (they were already well provided for by other members of the family), a trust to provide for his staff of servants with the remainder of his estate going to a charitable trust which he named "The McCune Foundation" in honor of his father and mother. He named the bank and his brother Marshall as executors of his estate and trustees of his trust, and provided that if Marshall were not living, "no successor executor or trustee need be appointed". The meaning of that phrase was unambiguous under Pennsylvania law: it meant that no successor could be appointed, even by the Orphans Court. (That was also the law of a majority of states in cases where there were multiple fiduciaries). His brother died after Charles had signed the will, but before Charles's death, leaving the bank as the sole executor and trustee.

The settlement of the estate kept me busy for several years. His home and farm in Moon Township were transferred to Montour Country Club, with restrictions on any future development of the property. The McCune Foundation was promptly started so that the Distribution Committee could carry on Charles's annual contributions, which amounted to about $3 million. While the bank was the sole trustee, Charles had provided that the charitable contributions would be made by a Distribution Committee of three persons: his brother, Kitty and John. The Committee members had the right to fill any vacancies. At the outset, there was a vacancy, as Marshall had died before Charles. Kitty and John made the distributions for a couple of years, but began to think that it might be wise to have a third member, if for nothing else to resolve any disagreement between them. John Echement encouraged them to appoint me, as I had been close to Charles and was well known to both of them, having represented each of them. So they asked me to fill that position, and I agreed to do so, and also told them that if any conflict arose in my position as counsel to the trustee and serving on the committee, I would resign.

One of the early decisions was whether to hire a staff to help in the grants. I supported that idea, suggesting we needed at least an executive director to handle the extensive paper work. While the two of them had had no difficulty in handling the early distributions, as they consisted largely in just continuing Charles's annual gifts, when the Foundation was fully funded the annual grants would exceed $10 million. They agreed, and I suggested several candidates, including Earland Carlson, the former president of Westminster College. He was chosen, and we found some space in the Commonwealth Building for him and a secretary.

Kitty died not long after that from cancer of the throat, no doubt brought on by her smoking habit. Dick had been named in Charles's will as her successor, and the Distribution Committee thereafter consisted of the three of us. We increased the foundation staff by adding a program officer to assist Earland and another clerical position. They did a good job of reviewing applications for grants, recommending ones that warranted further consideration, and thoroughly reviewing the financial stability and plans of the applicants. The Distribution Committee met three of four times a year and approved or rejected the recommendations of the staff for grants. Meetings were usually held in Pittsburgh, but at least once a year we held one in the Southwest (Dallas, Oklahoma City or Santa Fe) to accommodate John McCune, who did not care for flying.

We worked well together. The annual distributions increased to about $10 million as expected, and we moved toward making larger grants and reducing the number of small grants considered. The family did not want to publicize the name of the foundation, and refused to name buildings or scholarships, often being listed by the donee organizations as "Anonymous Foundation". However, I did not think it was wise to have the foundation be a mystery to the community, so on my recommendation after the first five years we published a five-year report of all grants made, and thereafter published an annual report. We tried to observe the grantor's wishes that we give preference to the charities he had supported during his lifetime, but we did not limit grants to that group.

There were two major blocks of stock in the Foundation: Texaco and Union National Corporation. The will directed the trustee not to sell these stocks in order to provide diversity, but the trustee could sell for other reasons. This direction was followed by the trustee, and the first problem arose when Texaco had a $10 billion verdict entered against it in a Texas lawsuit. The decision was outrageous, but it was affirmed by the Texas Supreme Court, and the company appealed to the U.S. Supreme Court. It was quite doubtful whether that court would intervene in the case. After much thought, and after consulting with the Distribution Committee, the trustee decided to sell about half of the Texaco stock and reinvest the proceeds in Exxon and Treasury bonds, again in accordance with the directions in the will. Texaco eventually reached a settlement and paid $4 billion, and went on with its business as though nothing had happened.

While it seemed like an important decision by the trustee at the time, it turned out that it didn't much matter. Both Texaco and Exxon did well in the following years.

The other block, a 20% interest in Union National, required more attention. The statutes regulating private foundations limited the foundation to owning not more that 20% of any company's stock. Included in that amount was stock owned by any related parties and their families, so the trustee was required to inquire annually as to the holdings of the Distribution Committee and their families. All parties agreed that it was in the foundation's best interest to continue to hold that stock, the largest block outstanding. So when more stock was issued, as in connection with any bank merger, the trustee would usually bring the holding back to the 20% limit. The Integra merger, which we will take up next, reduced that holding to about 10%, so when Integra redeemed the convertible debentures of Union National, the trustee exercised its right to convert its holding into stock. All of these actions were to the benefit of the charitable trust, as the value of the Foundation's assets increased from $86 million at inception to $400 million in the 1990s (even though $156 million had been distributed), with the Union National-Integra stock being the most profitable.

With the amount of money involved, perhaps it was inevitable that a serpent would enter this Garden of Eden of the McCune Foundation. In 1990, I suggested to John and Dick that we give some thought to our successors as members of the Distribution Committee, as we were all getting past retirement age. They both thought that each should add a son to the Distribution Committee, John choosing his eldest child (John R. McCune V), and Dick his youngest son, James, generally known as Jamie. Jamie was ambitious and wanted to be more than a member of the Distribution Committee, and conceived the idea that he should be a co-trustee with the bank. He read the will and concluded that there was a vacancy resulting from the death of Charles's brother, Marshall. Since the will said that the position need not be filled, he concluded that didn't prohibit the bank or the Orphans' Court from appointing one. When he brought up this idea to me, I pointed out that the law of Pennsylvania was clear, and that this language meant that nobody, not even the Court, could appoint a successor. He dismissed that idea as "one lawyer's opinion", and said he was sure he could find a lawyer with a different opinion. I suggested he consult George Lockhart, who was representing his grandfather's estate, or several other trust experts. Apparently he did, and apparently they all told him the same thing. But he did persuade his father and his Uncle John to write a letter to the Bank demanding that the bank appoint him as a co-trustee. They did so without consulting me. The bank asked for a written opinion from Buchanan Ingersoll, which was provided by Jim Ummer, pointing out why the bank could not appoint a successor and why there was no vacancy. Furthermore any attempt to do so would be opposed by the Attorney General, who has the duty of representing the charitable interests. I joined in the opinion.

However, Jamie eventually found a lawyer at Reed, Smith, Shaw & McClay by the name of Don Gerlach who was willing to try to get Jamie appointed as trustee, one way or another. He filed suit against the bank, and the Attorney General opposed this proposal, as predicted. After several months of pleadings and arguments before the Court, the petition was withdrawn. I deduced that even Gerlach saw that his position was fruitless. So they filed a new petition, this one seeking to have the bank removed as trustee, and appointing Pittsburgh National Bank as its successor. Jamie apparently thought if he could get a new corporate trustee, that trustee might go along with his proposition, or at least would do whatever he wanted to do. That petition was also opposed by the bank and the Attorney General, and after several revised petitions were filed and withdrawn, and after about two years of fruitless litigation, another petition was filed seeking damages from the bank and me for alleged breaches of trust. They wanted about $6 million from me. While flattered by the idea that anyone could collect that amount from me, I hired counsel to represent me, Buchanan Ingersoll being busy representing the bank.

I got an old friend, Dave Fawcett, a partner in Dickey, McCamie to represent me. Happily, I had an indemnification from Union National as a director and officer of it that resulted in the corporation paying my counsel fees. Dave, and his associates, Dorothy Davis and Roger Puz, filed an answer and preliminary objections on my behalf, asking that I be dismissed from the case. The judge quickly agreed, and I ceased to be a party. Gerlach tried to appeal that decision, but lost that also.

I won't go into all the details of the claims against the bank, as they filled seventy or more pages, but basically Gerlach was just fishing to find something that the bank had done wrong in the last ten or more years. The litigation went on for several years, but was finally tried. Gerlach called me as an adverse witness and I testified under cross-examination for three days. At the conclusion of my testimony, Gerlach rested his case. The Attorney General promptly moved that the petition be dismissed, and the Court quickly did so. That decision was affirmed by the Court *en banc*, and finally by the Superior Court of Pennsylvania. For a full reading of this opinion, see *In re McCune*, 705 A.2d 861 (Pa. Super. 1997). Out of all the judges who had heard or reviewed the case, all were unanimous: the claims were baseless.

So what was the result of these years of litigation? The Trustee spent about $2 million in counsel fees that were reimbursed from the trust corpus. In other words, charities paid for the case. The family was refused any reimbursement, so they either paid a similar amount themselves or found other sources. I thought they should be ashamed, but I am afraid they were not bothered by such niceties.

What thoughts do I now have about my decade of service to the McCune Foundation? On the whole, I enjoyed the experience. It was good to help a new foundation get started, and to work with Earland and his staff and the other members of the Distribution Committee. We gave away more than $100 million to charities during that time and I think our choices of recipients were sound. My memories are positive, and only slightly tainted by the foolish litigation that ended that period.

24

Armstrong World Industries

I previously noted my joining the Armstrong Board in 1976. I enjoyed the experience of serving on this board for the next twenty years. There were a number of reasons for this, and let me mention two. A lawyer generally deals with clients with a problem, or a single project like an acquisition, and when that job is done, the client goes on doing business as before and the lawyer moves on to some other problem. In short, we lawyers see the problems, and tend to miss the regular routine, successful part of a business. A lawyer for a bank, for example, might deal with all the problem loans and forget that most of the loans are paid on schedule without his help.

Board membership gave me an appreciation of the business side of a large company. There are rhythms to it: the annual planning and budgeting, the measuring of performance against the plans, the development of new products and new ventures, and reviews of the corporate personnel, to mention a few. Armstrong had a strong group of capable officers, and an interesting and distinguished board, so the work was enjoyable. Our meetings were held at the headquarters in Lancaster, with one or two meetings a year held at one of the company's plants in the United States. I particularly enjoyed the plant tours, and seeing the production of flooring or ceilings or whatever product was made there. In the early years, the meetings were held almost monthly, but as time went on the meetings became less frequent, with five or six per year. I served on several board committees, but the two I spent most time on were the audit and pension committees. During this period the management recommended that the company name be changed from "Armstrong Cork" to "Armstrong World Industries" as the company no longer had much to do with the original business of cutting corks for bottles. The board approved, but I rather hated to see the historical name disappear.

The second reason I found the experience enjoyable was the association with the Armstrong people and the other directors. There were too many of them to mention individually, but several directors stand out. For example, Paul Lyet was a role model for me as an outside director. He was chairman of Sperry-Rand at the time, and an accountant by background. He was among the most knowledgeable of us, and his familiarity with all aspects of running a large company was always impressive. I have a photo of him, Jim Binns and me taken for one of the annual reports, hanging in my present office, and I still regret his untimely passing from cancer shortly after he retired.

Eric Walker, former President of Penn State and then an officer of Alcoa, was another favorite. Eric was an engineer and scientist by training, and he was influential in supporting the development of technology at Armstrong. I often discussed academic matters with him, and his pithy observations were always entertaining. Once when we were talking about student-faculty ratios he pointed out how subjective such measures are. He said "Never suppose that you get the ratio by dividing the number of faculty into the number of students." His point was that you can get whatever ratio you want in how you define "faculty" and who you count as "students".

Bill Ellingsworth was President of AT&T at the time of its split-up. He retired shortly after that, and related that when he went back to his office a few months later to talk to his successor, the receptionist asked him his name. He claimed that he had set a new record in going from "Who's Who" to "Who's He?" Naomi Albanese was the Dean of the Home Economics Department at North Carolina University, and since she was a graduate of Muskingum College, a sister college of Westminster, our common ground fostered a warm friendship.

Rocky Caldwell was one of the Company officers who were directors. He invited me to go on a sailing weekend with him and several friends on Chesapeake Bay. Rocky and several of his buddies were former naval officers, and all good sailors. We had a fleet of about five or six sloops, and had a grand time sailing in the daytime and partying in the evenings. We did that for several years and on at least two occasions it was graduation weekend at Annapolis. We would anchor in Annapolis harbor and watch the Navy's Blue Angels put on their show. I was tempted to duck every time they flew over, as it seemed that they were just barely above the masts of the ships in the harbor.

There were many other good directors, Phil Samper and Frank Breeze among them, and each brought a broad business experience to bear on Armstrong's issues. Barbara Franklin joined the board, but before long was drafted by Ronald Reagan as his Secretary of Commerce. My apologies to all I have failed to mention.

I also greatly admired the Presidents of Armstrong, sound and moral businessmen all. Jim Binns was President when I first became a director, and he was a brilliant and charismatic leader. He was succeeded on his retirement by Harry Jensen, a quieter but equally warm and friendly person. I thought it was Harry's ill fortune to guide the company during a period of economic recession, but he never complained about that. Joe Jones was his successor, a graduate of Virginia Tech and a former resident from a town near Farmville, Virginia. On the eve of the surrender at Appomatox in 1865, General Lee stayed in the home of one of his ancestors, and General Grant in the home of another. Joe had the good fortune to enjoy several years of economic prosperity and the company thrived during this time.

Joe was succeeded by Bill Adams who had a more intellectual and analytical approach to business. The problems of asbestos, described hereafter, hung over his presidency, and he retired fairly early. I thought about retiring about this time, but decided I should stay on while his successor, George Lorch, got his administration going.

All of these men and women were wonderful friends, and I continue to treasure the memories of my associations with them.

There was one problem that plagued the Company for most of the years that I was a director, and that was the intractable problem of asbestosis claims. At first it was only a small black cloud on the horizon. During World War II, Armstrong had contracted with the U.S. government to spray asbestos on Navy vessels being built at a brisk pace. The asbestos was the best known fire retardant, and no doubt saved many lives during combat. However, scientific research during the 1960s established that asbestos fibers were the cause of the lung disease named asbestosis. The condition could also lead to fatal cancer growth in the lungs. The asbestosis disease can take decades to develop, so the results of the exposure may take up to forty years to manifest.

The U.S. Government took the cowardly position that it could not be held liable for damages to the workers involved, claiming its sovereign immunity from suit. That left the companies that had lawfully carried out the government contracts to bear the liability. Armstrong had substantial liability insurance that we believed to be adequate to handle the claims, but Armstrong thus became one of the dozen or so companies named in every asbestosis suit. Armstrong had also sold pipe insulation for many years containing asbestos fibers, and asbestos made up the backing for the vinyl flooring made by the Company. Plaintiffs were not required to show that their asbestosis was the result of any particular exposure, so all companies having anything to do with asbestos were liable without proof of cause.

Johns Manville, which mined and sold asbestos to other companies, was the first of the defendants to declare bankruptcy. One by one the other defendants followed into bankruptcy. But we were financially strong and our insurance coverage seemed adequate to protect us. However, the asbestos claims continued to grow, and various efforts were made to deal with the claims administratively, but none were effective. An attempt was made to dispose of all claims, present and future, through a class action brought in the Federal courts, but the Supreme Court held that the class action statute did not permit this. The Federal courts were becoming clogged with all the claims, and all appeals to Congress to create an administrative procedure to handle asbestos claims fell on deaf ears. More accurately, the lawyers handling the plaintiffs' cases had become so wealthy that they were a powerful lobbying force in Congress and in presidential elections to block any reform. They were among the biggest financial supporters of Bill Clinton, for example.

Larry Pulkrabek was Armstrong's General Counsel, and he did a heroic job of handling the asbestos cases and the claims against the insurance companies. At the time of my retirement from Armstrong he still had high hopes for the class action case. Sadly, he was forced to retire for health reasons not too long after that, and the Company lost his several decades of experience in handling these cases. Finally, in 2001, the Company, finding itself one of the few surviving defendants in these cases, gave up and went into a reorganization under Chapter 11 of the Bankruptcy law, thereby wiping out all the shareholder equity in the Company.

I will admit to feeling some bitterness for the failure of our entire legal system in the handling of asbestosis claims. Congress certainly failed, the common law tort system was totally inadequate to deal with these claims, and the asbestosis victims have seen most of the money produced in the litigation and bankruptcies go to the plaintiffs' lawyers. Hurray for them. I can only hope that a good company like Armstrong will return from the reorganization free of future claims and become again the great company it once was.

25

Integra Financial Corporation

Life was going well in 1988. I had been chairman of Union National Corporation for about five years, we had just about settled the litigation over the fraudulent letters of credit, and we were the proud owners of five Western Pennsylvania banks. The McCune Foundation dispute was several years in the future. But as we tried to acquire more banks, we frequently ran into conflict with Pennbancorp, a bank holding company the same size as us. Their banks were located north and south of our set of banks, and they had little presence in Pittsburgh, where we were strong. We had talked in the past about the possibility of merging the two bank holding companies, but nothing had ever come of those conversations.

One day in May of that year, I had a call from Bill Roemer, the chairman of Pennbancorp, asking me to have lunch with him at the Duquesne Club. I was happy to do so, and found that what he had on his mind was a serious exploration of the possibilities of a merger of our two companies. I agreed that it was time to do so: either it would prove attractive to both of us or we should quit thinking about it.

At the same time, we had been indirectly approached by PNC to be acquired by them, and Equibank was hoping we might acquire them. I talked briefly to Tom O'Brien, chairman of PNC, but he did not seem interested enough to offer the substantial premium I thought we deserved. Equibank had many financial problems and seemed to be too big a risk for us to take on. I discussed all three of these possibilities with the Union National board, and they agreed that we should pursue the discussions with Pennbancorp.

We held several meetings with the principal officers of the two companies. For Pennbancorp, it was Bill Roemer, Len Carroll and Chuck Skillington. For us, it was George Kesel, John Echement, Bill Walker and myself. The geographic fit was obvious: a merger would put together the best retail banking system in Western Pennsylvania, with deposits greater than those of either PNC or Mellon in that area. Our balance sheets were nearly identical in size and the market capitalizations of both companies were similar. The principal difference in our assets was that we had a portfolio of commercial real estate loans, and Pennbancorp had a portfolio of bank stocks (including a substantial holding of our stock). Both asset classifications added a different degree of risk than the rest of the balance sheets. After several months of study and discussions, we all thought that if the remaining issues could be resolved we might make a deal.

Of course, the two remaining issues were the most difficult: first, who would be the management of the new company, and finally, what would be the exchange ratio for the two stocks. Bill and his board were adamant that he should be the CEO of the new company; that was fine with me, but George thought he should have that job, at least at the outset. Bill had suggested that I be the Chairman of the Board, and George and the other officers be Vice Chairman. That idea did not appeal to George. I suggested to both sets of officers that if we couldn't agree on this, both sets of officers should be shot and gotten out of the way of a good merger. This didn't receive much applause.

I had a call from Joe Harvey, an old friend and a retired chairman of one of Pennbancorp's banks, First Seneca, and a director of Pennbancorp, asking me to have breakfast with him. Joe said that there didn't seem to be any good solution to the CEO conflict, and that they, the Pennbancorp board, would not go forward unless Bill got that job. He asked if I would be willing to give up the Chairman title, which might satisfy George. That would leave me as a Vice Chairman, which didn't appeal to me, but I told him I would do so in order to make the merger happen. However, I told him that I wouldn't stay long in the Vice Chairman position, as retirement was beginning to look more attractive to me.

So it was finally agreed that this would be the new team, albeit with some reluctance on George's part. The remaining issue was what the exchange rate should be. We were being advised by the investment banking firm of Keefe, Bruyette & Woods, and their principal man was Andy Senchak. Andy had worked on all of our earlier mergers (investment bankers give "fairness opinions" to the shareholders of the banks involved), and Andy had become a friend. We agreed to propose an exchange ratio of 1.27:1, with each share of Union National getting 1.27 shares of the new company, and Pennbancorp getting 1 share. Bill Roemer and his advisor came back with a proposed ratio of 1.05 to 1, which didn't come close to our objective. Bill came up some, and I agreed to lower our ratio to 1.24. That didn't sell too well, but I dug in my heels and said I wouldn't go any lower. However, since Pennbancorp owned a substantial number of shares in our company, I was quite willing to have those shares be paid the same ratio as ours, which brought their share up to 1.05 shares of the new company. That finally resulted in a deal, and we soon signed a contract that was approved by both boards of directors. The negotiations over the terms of the contract were intense, with Buchanan Ingersoll representing us and Kirkpatrick Lockhart representing Pennbancorp.

We called a press conference for the day the boards approved the deal, and had the pleasure to announce this to the radio and TV media late in the afternoon. The news was well received, but a few bankers who had hoped to merge with one or another of us were disappointed, and a few shareholders who hoped that either of us would sell out to some bigger bank for a premium were disappointed. The announcement was in November, 1988.

That began a one-year period of fairly hard work to put this company together. We had to agree on a board of directors, and we settled on a slate of twenty directors, ten coming from each of our companies. It was a good board, and when I look at the photo of us in the 1988 Annual Report of Integra Financial Corporation (for that was the name we had chosen), I feel proud to have been included in their company.[1]

The name was not an easy choice. It is a common delusion that corporate names can be easily chosen by anyone with imagination, but the contrary is true. Most names are not available, someone else having already used one's imaginative choice, or because it is geographically limiting (like *Union National Bank of Pittsburgh*) or for a variety of other reasons (e.g., we didn't want to use any of our existing bank names). So we hired a firm that specializes in selecting corporate

---

1.   Bob Eberly, Joe Harvey, Bob Paul, Tom Gillespie, John Britton, Carl Doverspike, Hank Suhr, Jim Feeney, Bill Hirt, Jim Beckwith, Al Duval, Walter Greenleaf, Rod Hornbake, John Koedel, Dick Edwards, Stan Gumberg, Miff McBride, and of course, George, Bill and I.

names (yes, that is a branch of the public relations industry), which developed a list of potential names that might be available, and we eventually settled on Integra Financial Corporation. The usual legal search did not turn up any conflicts, and we announced the new name.

Shortly after the announcement I received a letter from an IBM employee savings union in suburban New York stating they had already registered the name "Integra" for their brokerage subsidiary, and that we had better discuss this conflict. I went to visit the CEO, named Al Menard, accompanied by our trademark lawyer, Paul Beck. We talked about the possibility that because of our geographic separation there would be no conflict. I couldn't convince myself that we would accept any territorial limits, and Menard was certain that we would eventually conflict. He proposed that we buy their rights to the name, and proposed a method of arriving at a price. We were each to submit a written offer on the same day, and then negotiate from there. After discussion with our management committee, we decided that it would be worth $200,000 to keep the name. But we didn't want to pay that much, so we made an offer of $75,000 and the same day Menard's letter indicated he would accept $115,000. He came to Pittsburgh, and said he would split the difference, and we agreed. We acquired the right to the name, and also his prior use of the name (predating our use by six months). That prior use later proved effective in stopping another company (this in Canada) from its use of the name.

In June of 1988, George Kesel, Bill Roemer, Chuck Skillington and I flew to London to present our story to a group of British bank analysts (sponsored by Keefe Bruyette), and went on to Glasgow to meet potential Scottish investors. As I noted in a diary for that year: "The trip was interesting and enjoyable, and a good learning experience in investor relations for the new Integra management."

The most contentious issue before the management group that year was the question of consolidation of our eight banks. Both the Pennbank and Union National managements wanted to make a decision on the consolidation and present it to the board prior to the merger. It was anticipated that we would eventually reduce the number to three banks, one in Pittsburgh, one in Erie, and the third in Uniontown. The three banks would all do business under the Integra name, and the names and boards of directors of all eight banks would disappear. Of course, the boards of the three banks would be made up of directors taken from the old banks, but only a fraction of those directors would be retained.

I was adamantly opposed to doing anything along these lines until after the merger was consummated and we had had a year or two of experience in our new holding company. The elimination of existing banks would be a sore subject with the directors, employees, depositors and borrowers of each of these banks, and we had enough problems in 1988 without adding this to our plate. I finally expressed my views in a letter to George and Bill, which succeeded in annoying everyone concerned. However, they eventually came around to my viewpoint, and the issue was shelved until after the merger. I later expressed the view that getting everyone mad at me had the salutary effect of uniting the managements so they did not waste time fighting among themselves.

Eventually the year came to an end, and we had succeeded in selling off the branches required by the Justice Department, had gotten shareholder approval by each of the holding companies, had the approval of the Comptroller of the Currency, and the merger could be completed. However, we were told that we could not merge until the branch sales had been closed, and that was going to require several more months. We had a substantial tax problem if the merger could not be completed in January, so I spent considerable time in talking to the Fed in Cleveland, in Washington, and even in Richmond (which had jurisdiction over a few Gallatin bank branches being sold to a West Virginia bank), pleading for permission to close prior to the branch sale closings. They eventually relented, and we were able to put the branches in escrow pending the closing of those sales. Happily, our merger was completed in January, 1989, and we finally became Integra Financial Corporation.

26

Westminster College

From 1976 on, I served as a Trustee of Westminster. Glenn had been on the board for several years, and following his death in 1975 they asked me to take his place. Earland Carlson was the President at that time, and Judge John Miller was the Chairman of the Board. The two of them worked well together, but after a few years the Judge died, and Bob Lauterbach was elected Chair. Carlson and Miller had enjoyed a productive relationship, but Earland and Bob Lauterbach were not so compatible. After a particularly unpleasant incident involving a student, Earland resigned, and Bob announced that he would take over as Interim President. He and his wife, Jane, moved into the President's house, and that began a troubled period in Westminster's history. That story has been told in more detail in Paul Gamble's history of the College, so I won't repeat it here. Relationships between the Faculty and the Trustees sank to a new low, and before long the Faculty were passing resolutions demanding Bob's removal as President. The trustees finally felt it was time for a new administration, so Bob and Tom Mansell resigned as Chair and Vice Chairman. Jack Hoey, the President of Peoples Gas was elected as the new Chair.

I had been perturbed by the conflict, as both Earland and Bob were friends of mine, and in fact Earland had come to work with the McCune Foundation. I presided at a farewell dinner for Bob, and truthfully thanked him for all he had done for his Alma Mater. But there was a feeling of relief that he had finally quit the premises, which I'm sure he shared.

I arranged to have lunch with Jack Hoey shortly after that to tell him that it was time for me to resign as well. I had served for several terms as a trustee, was tired of the struggle, and I thought I deserved a rest. Jack told me that this would not do, as he had something else in mind for me. He told me that it wasn't easy for him to take on the role of Chairman of the Board (he wasn't even an alum), and he expected me to take the job as Chair of a search committee for a new President. It was the last thing in the world I wanted to do, but Jack was and is a man of quiet persuasion, a devout Christian, and a person to whom it is difficult to say "no". I thought about it and eventually agreed to take on the job, with more than a little reluctance.

We put together a search committee, consisting of four trustees and one faculty member. I did not have the patience to deal with the usual large academic search committee with representatives of every constituency: students, faculty, alumni, parents, trustees, etc. And there was a sense of urgency to find someone as quickly as possible. Jerry Boone was acting as Interim President and, with Jack's help, kept the institution operating. I also insisted that we have a professional headhunter, and we chose Boyden Associates, with Wade Close in their Pittsburgh office as our contact.

We looked at a number of candidates, but could not agree on any one of them. In the process of searching, Wade suggested I meet with the President of Alma College, a Presbyterian college in Michigan. His name was Oscar Remick, and while he was not a candidate, Wade thought this was the type of person we needed. I arranged to meet with Dr. Remick in the Washington airport when he was on a trip to the Capitol. After a two-hour meeting, I returned rather dejected, telling Ginnie I had met the ideal person for the job, but that he was not interested in it. But he had given me one clue that led to a slim hope: when asked what would ever cause him to leave Alma, he said quite simply that he had always tried to do what he was called by God to do, and that was what had led to his various career choices. I had responded rather modestly that I wasn't sure I had any warrant to speak for God.

After thinking about this, I decided I had been too modest. I was as likely a messenger of God as anyone, and if God wanted Oscar Remick to be President of Westminster College, it would happen. I looked up the story of Samuel in the Bible, as that might provide some insight into people who found themselves called by the Almighty. Shortly after that I called Oscar on the telephone and asked him if he was familiar with 1 Samuel, Chapter 3, verse 9.[1] He laughed and said "No, but I will be." I suggested he read and commit the message to heart.

---

1.   The verse contains the advice Eli gave to Samuel when God called him. He was to answer "Speak, Lord, for your servant is listening."

It was many months before Oscar heard that call, and only after many lunches and dinners with Jack Hoey, me, the trustees, and finally a trip to the College to meet the faculty. One fine day he called Jack and me on a conference call and said he had decided to accept the challenge of the Presidency of Westminster. I can still feel the sense of relief and joy that I experienced that day.[2]

Oscar did not let me forget my obligation to him, and when Jack's term as Chairman of the Board was finished, I was told to accept that job. Joe Mack and I had persuaded the Board to revise the by-laws to provide that a person could hold the position of Chair for not more than three years, and that has been the rule ever since. So I served my three years, and it was a pleasure to work with Oscar and watch him build up a new administrative staff, work with the faculty, improve relations with alumni, raise money and do all the things a successful college president must do. Near the end of my term, Oscar decreed that it was time for a capital fund drive, and since I would be unemployed as Chair, I would be the chairman of that.

I was succeeded as Chair by my old friend and classmate, Don Wiley, who was then General Counsel to the Heinz Company. Don and his wife, Josie, have a home in Chatham, Mass. (as well as homes in Pittsburgh and Florida), and we see them frequently every Summer. For several years, Don has invited me to play in the annual invitational golf tournament at Eastward Ho! Country Club in Chatham, and we have enjoyed those outings. Nobody would mistake either of us for a serious golfer, and we have always been assigned to the highest handicap flight in the tournament. However, we have won the flight or placed second or third most years. Alas, in 2002 we ended up being the worst of the worst, so perhaps we are getting a little ancient for such serious golf.

But, I digress. The capital campaign took about five years, but we reached our goal of $35 million, which was almost three times what we had raised in the last campaign in the 1970's. Chairmen are largely figureheads in such events, and the heavy lifting is mostly done by the college President. Oscar was quite adept at

---

2.   Needless to say, there was disappointment and outrage in Michigan. The Governor of the state wrote urging him to change his mind, as of course did the trustees of Alma. I felt some counter-weight was appropriate, and I got Dick Thornburgh, who was then Governor of Pennsylvania, to write him a letter welcoming him to Pennsylvania. Oscar observed wryly that he could guess who put him up to that.

that, and his large circle of friends in Pennsylvania by then equaled the large circle he had enjoyed in Michigan.

In due time, Oscar reached retirement age and returned to his home near Ellsworth, Maine. He went back to teaching at the University of Maine and also at the Bangor Theological Seminary, where he became the academic dean. We stayed in touch, and since we both were on the board of a privately owned company named Tango, Inc., owned by Scott Beck, we got to see each other frequently. Alas, after returning from a trip to New Zealand, I had a phone call from him telling me the news that he had been diagnosed with bone cancer. He was beginning the chemotherapy for that when I got a call from Emma, his wife, that he was failing fast. I flew to Bangor and had a chance to talk to him briefly at the hospital, but he died the following day. I do sorely miss him, one of the best friends a person could ever have.

I cannot leave this piece of history of Westminster without paying tribute to those who succeeded Oscar. We were fortunate to find an outstanding new President in Tom Williamson. Along with my successors as Chair, Don Wiley, Scott Beck, Bob Gardner, Len Carroll and George Berlin, he and they have led the college to new and greater heights than I could have dreamed of when I first went on the board. They were so gracious as to confer on me an honorary degree, Doctor of Laws, at Commencement in 2000, and I treasure that memory along with all the other memories of my Alma Mater.

27

Dinner at the White House

In the spring of 1987, we got an unusual surprise. We received in the mail an engraved invitation saying that the President and Mrs. Reagan requested the pleasure of our company at dinner on Friday, April 24, 1987. My first suspicion was that this was some elaborate hoax by one of my acquaintances, but it appeared genuine and we were to respond to the Social Secretary of the White House, "giving date of birth and social security number". So we did, and got further instructions about attire (business suits).

We were still rather puzzled about our inclusion, but we duly showed up at the White House gate and after showing identification and having our names checked off the list, we were sent to the front door. We stood there for a few seconds expecting it to open up, but the Marine guard standing next to the door said "Push". We did, and were greeted inside by an aide who took our coats and escorted us to an elevator that took us to the second floor where the private quarters of the President are located. We walked down a long hall, and there was a tall man who looked just like Ronald Reagan. It was Ronald Reagan! He greeted us warmly, asked me if I were related to his favorite General from World War II, and I gave him the usual answer "Not on this side of the Atlantic". He apologized for having to entertain his guests at cocktails in the corridor, because the staff had lit a fire in the Lincoln Room, and the room had filled up with smoke. He thought the house was in need of some repairs. He introduced us to Nancy, and showed us a rare gift from the Chinese government, a framed silk tapestry that could be viewed from both sides. Ginnie had heard about the technique, and we were photographed with him examining this curiosity. We got a signed copy of the photo later, and it proudly hangs in my office.

The reason for the invitation became clear after we talked to a young man from the Hoover Institute at Stanford. The purpose of the dinner was to raise funds for the Ronald Reagan Presidential Library, which the President thought should be privately funded rather than publicly. I had met some of the staff of the Hoover Institute a year or so before when the McCune Foundation had made a grant to them. I was the face of that Foundation to them, and they had also invited the head of the Pew Foundation in Philadelphia. There were several Hoover folks there, including Glenn Campbell, its director, and the largest collection of billionaires I will ever see in one room. Walter Annenberg, Kirk Kerkorian (who had just flown in from Europe on his private jet), Mr. Stone, an insurance tycoon from Chicago, and Malcolm Forbes, the publisher of Forbes magazine. I had read enough about him to ask how his most recent motorcycle trip had gone, a subject he was happy to discuss. There were a few other business men and wives present, and after cocktails, the President led us into the family dining room.

There were four or five tables with eight at each table. I was seated at Nancy Reagan's table, and Ginnie at the President's table. Nancy spent most of her time talking to an old friend from Hollywood, but I got to talk to the other guests. I was seated next to the Pew Foundation head, and we had something in common to talk about. Mrs. Annenberg was also at our table. Ginnie, at her table, had a delightful conversation with President Reagan. He must have done his homework, because he started to talk to her about genealogy, her favorite pastime. She had been the president of the Pittsburgh Genealogical Society a few years before that, and the FBI perhaps had checked that out. Ginnie was seated next to Walter Annenberg, and she asked him if he were a wine connoisseur, and he said no but he liked to cook and made his own spaghetti sauce, which he described in detail to her.

It was an excellent dinner, but the most memorable thing to me was the wine, a 1962 Chateau Lafite-Rothschild. I thought it a little strange that the former Governor of California was serving a French wine. Ginnie reported that Mr. Annenberg, who seemed quite at home in the White House, asked for a second helping of soup. I, on the other hand, was happy to accept a second glass of the wine, a vintage I would not be likely to encounter again.

After dinner, Mr. Reagan gave a short talk about his plans for a Presidential Library, and why he thought it was appropriate for him not to ask for money from the taxpayers but from his friends. We then adjourned to the Lincoln Room, which had since been aired out, for coffee and cakes, and informal conversation. Ronald Reagan was in his element here. A born raconteur, he told one funny story after another and seemed to thoroughly enjoy it. At one point, Ginnie was standing near him, and he put his arm around her to draw her into the circle. She thought about this, and decided it would be her only chance to put her arm around a President, so she did. He didn't mind, but I thought Nancy looked a bit chilly.

The best laugh we had that evening came at our departure. Most of the guests were leaving in their limousines, but we were staying at the Willard Hotel, only a block away, and had walked down to the White House. It was a rainy evening, and we had on our raincoats and Ginnie put a scarf over he head to protect her hairdo. When we got to the gate, the guard asked us for our passes. I looked puzzled and said we didn't have any, we had been guests at the dinner. The guard apologized, saying, "Oh, we thought you were part of the staff". We stood on the curb outside and laughed. I said "Welcome back to the real world!"

Yes, the McCune Foundation did make a contribution to the Library, but only after I explained to the person in charge of fund raising for the Library that perhaps they had invited the wrong person from the foundation, as I was the only non-family member on the Distribution Committee, which might make it a little delicate. So shortly after that, John McCune, Dick Edwards and Earland Carlson were invited to lunch at the White House, but they didn't have as much fun as we had.

One final footnote: Ginnie, ever the chef, had loved the cold soufflé with strawberry sauce served for dessert, so she wrote to the White House Social Secretary and asked if she could have the recipe. She got a polite reply saying the chef said that the recipe was so complicated he could not possibly put it on paper as he had created it specially for this particular dinner. Who says you can't keep secrets in Washington?

28

Bank Consulting Associates

Getting back to banking, I spent the year of 1989 as Vice Chairman of our new Integra Financial. It was largely a period of getting organized. We moved our temporary executive offices into PPG Plaza, taking over a floor of Building 4. It was an interesting year in getting to know the directors of the three Pennbancorp banks, and getting to know the new group of officers and people of all eight of our banks.

There was an incident early in the year that I found interesting. I had called on the president of a bank in Morgantown, W. Va. a couple of times in the previous years to see if they might be interested in joining Union National Corp. His name was Ed Skriner, and he wasn't interested in selling, but said he would keep us in mind if the situation changed. Integra happened to own a block of stock in that bank, amounting to about 5% of the outstanding stock. One day in 1989 Chuck Skillington came into my office with the announcement that Morgantown had agreed to sell to Huntingdon Bankshares for $28 per share. We both thought that was inadequate and that we would have been happy to pay more for the bank. All the other Integra officers were away that day, but we managed to get Bill Roemer by phone and proposed that we send a letter to the directors of the Morgantown bank opposing the sale and offering to pay a higher price. He agreed, and I fired off a letter by fax to that effect.

Our guess was that Huntingdon had only signed a letter of intent, subject to approval by both boards when they had a definitive agreement prepared later, as that was fairly normal practice in bank mergers. We immediately got a letter from Huntingdon claiming they had a binding agreement, and threatening to sue us if we interfered with their deal. I answered and said if that were the case, just send us a copy of the agreement. They refused, and we knew they were bluffing.

We immediately retained lawyers to help us in our effort, getting Skadden Arps from New York, which had considerable experience in this type of litigation. We also got Kirkpatrick Lockhart in Pittsburgh as local counsel (Buchanan Ingersoll couldn't represent us because of a conflict). They advised us to file suit immediately in the Federal Court in Pittsburgh, as the other party would try to sue us before a friendly judge in West Virginia. The lawyers moved fast, and we had a complaint filed quickly and succeeded in serving it on Huntingdon before they could do anything in West Virginia. According to counsel, they were somewhat taken aback when served with our complaint because they were filing that same day in West Virginia. Sure enough, they had a friendly judge who immediately issued a preliminary injunction ordering us to cease and desist. Judge Cohill in Pittsburgh immediately quashed that as his court had prior jurisdiction.

That forced the hand of the Morgantown board of directors. They decided they had to conduct an auction, giving both Huntingdon and us a chance to bid, and providing us with an opportunity for due diligence with their books and records. We had no illusions that the auction would be fair: they could always give Huntingdon a second look after we bid. So we came up with the highest number we could justify which was about $32 per share and sent it in. In the meantime, we kept buying up the Morgantown stock on the market at prices from $28 and up, and eventually accumulated just less than 10% of their stock, which is all we could legally own.

We both submitted our bids on the same day, and nothing was heard for about 24 hours. Then, not unexpectedly, Huntingdon announced that they had signed a definitive agreement with Morgantown for a price about five cents more than we had offered. We had lost the girl, but we got a nice consolation prize. We made a several million dollar profit on the stock. Huntingdon agreed to buy our stock if we would agree to vote in favor of the merger, and we did.

I decided that there should be a little more fun in this, so I went to the Morgantown shareholders meeting to vote our stock. I announced that we were going to vote in favor of the merger, but I had a few questions to ask. The first was whether the original agreement was merely a letter of intent, and not a binding agreement. The chairman told me that was correct, and I pointed out that the Huntingdon press release had been false and misleading, and they should call this to their attention.

The second question was whether their investment bankers had given the board a "fairness opinion" as to the original $28 price. The answer to that was also "yes", and the investment bankers present could only glower when I pointed out how wrong they had been.

The final question was whether, at the time the bids were open, our bid was the highest. The answer again was "yes" but then Huntingdon had been allowed to increase their bid. I pointed out that we would never trust their investment bankers to conduct a fair auction in the future, but we were glad that the shareholders had received an additional $100 million dollars for their bank. I left the meeting laughing, as most of the shareholders were thanking me for seeing they got a fair price, and the directors were torn between thanks, as shareholders, and resentment for making them look so dumb as directors. Needless to say, there were a number of people at Huntingdon who would have cheerfully shot me.

I enjoyed the year with Integra, but as I had reached the age of 62 there was no real need for me to stay at Integra, so I announced my retirement at the end of the year. The board had a nice dinner to celebrate this occasion, and presented me with a fine painting by my old college classmate, Chuck Pitcher (Ginnie had made the selection). It is entitled "Sycamores" and now hangs in our home on Cape Cod. I was happy to stay on the board of directors, and was made Chairman of the Executive Committee of the board.

One of my diversions during these years was the ancient game of golf. I belonged to Chartiers Country Club, and we had a regular foursome consisting of Ray Brown, general counsel to Mobay, my partner, Bruce McCullough, who later became a Federal bankruptcy judge, and Leonard Carroll, the President of Integra. We fought many fierce battles, sometimes wagering such large sums as $2.00, changing partners each time we played. Our games took us on many travels: Scotland, Ireland, Hilton Head, Cape Cod, Arizona and various other spots. We would not be confused with good golfers. Bruce came up with the name for the group: "*The Dukes of Dork*". It fit, but we had wonderful times and still do.

I thought I was a bit young to start hanging around home annoying my wife, so I went back to Buchanan Ingersoll as "Counsel". I could not get enthusiastic about going into law practice again, so I formed a group to do bank consulting work and adopted the name "Bank Consulting Associates". It was a fine group, including lawyers (Bruce McCullough, Bill Newlin and Pam Rollings), real estate expertise (Stan Gumberg), an investment banker (Dave Hunter), and two CPA's from Ernst & Young (Modispacher and Haunschild). Needless to say, none of the members gave up their day jobs, as this was just a way of possibly marketing their services. It was a nice idea, but had one weakness that soon became apparent: I was still on the board of Integra and was chairing the Executive Committee. Integra had already acquired a reputation as a bank acquirer, and small banks in Western Pennsylvania looked on me as the advance spy. As a result, I soon learned there was little prospect of representing small banks and savings institutions in Western Pennsylvania.

I must mention some further connections with my friend, Stanley Gumberg. When we were both on the Union National Board, I persuaded him to join the Westminster Board. We had no Jewish board members, and it was time to broaden our membership. He was instrumental in getting his neighbor, Bishop Donald Wuerl, the head of the Pittsburgh Catholic diocese to join the Westminster board. So when he asked me to go on the board of Montefiore Hospital, of which he was Chairman, I could hardly refuse. It was an interesting experience, and when UPMC took over Montefiore, he negotiated an arrangement whereby the buyer would pay $75 million to a new foundation, named the Jewish Healthcare Foundation. The board of Montefiore became the first board of that foundation, so I had the honor of being the only non-Jewish member of that foundation. It was again interesting to be in at the creation of another major Pittsburgh foundation.

Getting back to Bank Consulting Associates, I did pick up some business in Central and Eastern Pennsylvania, and stayed busy at Buchanan Ingersoll for two more years, but when the period was up, I retired. I continued to do some consulting work from my home office, including acting as an expert witness in banking and trust litigation, and continued with arbitration work with the New York Stock Exchange and with the NASD.

In 1996, Integra agreed to merge with National City Corporation from Cleveland, and that ended my service as a bank director. I was due for reelection to the Armstrong Board that same year, and since I would be required to retire in two more years by reason of age, I decided that this would be a good time to leave that post. The Armstrong directors had a nice retirement party for me at the Lancaster Opera House that both Ginnie and I enjoyed. For the first time, I was really retired and it felt good.

29

Kids and Quackers

Life gets mixed up, doesn't it? At least trying to recount it in any chronological order does. So let me go back to 1983. Susan was about to graduate from Chicago Law School, and had spent the previous summer clerking at a Chicago law firm and also at Buchanan Ingersoll. She called me one winter day to tell me she was not going to accept the job offer from Buchanan. I assumed she had decided to practice in Chicago, but she said, "No, I have decided to go with Kirkpatrick Lockhart." That baffled me, as she hadn't had any clerkship with them. When I asked why, she said she didn't want to practice in the same firm as her father and her husband. That completely mystified me, until she told me that she had been dating Dan Altman, a junior partner in my firm, who had been working on the Recruiting Committee. We had had no clue about this so it was a complete surprise to both her father and mother. Dan had recruited her, all right, but as a spouse rather than as an associate. I did suggest to him that there was a doctrine in the law called "seizing a corporate opportunity", but neither of them were impressed with my legal theory. So, in August of 1983, there was another wedding at Southminster and reception at Chartiers, and we had three married children. Dan was from Uniontown, where his father, named Wesley, but known as "Hap",was an architect. He had been a World War II officer in the Navy. Hap and his wife Millys became a part of our extended family, and *vice versa*.

Before getting on to the subject of grandchildren, let us pass to the next and last wedding, in November 1986. Laura had been working as a social worker, and in the course of her employment had met a young fellow named Christopher Norton. They dated for a while, and one night Laura discussed with her parents the possibility of marriage with a young man who was Catholic. We raised no objection if they both had thought through any conflicts that this might raise between them. They attended counseling with his church, and Laura was content to raise her children in the Catholic faith. So our blessings were unreserved, and the ceremony at Southminster was attended by both a Presbyterian minister and a Catholic priest. A word about the latter: he was, and is, Jim Heft and he was then the Provost at Dayton University, where Chris had graduated. He had been Chris's favorite professor, and he is a warm, witty and blessedly intellectual companion. We are happy to count him as a close family friend. Chris's father had previously died, so we never had the good fortune to meet him, but his mother, Nancy and her present husband, Bob Daufenbach, are neighbors and share in the pleasure of watching our grandchildren grow up.

And speaking of grandchildren, it is about time we do. Barb and Niels were the first to marry, and the first to present us with a fine young grandson named Erik. He has since graduated from Washington & Lee University and is profitably employed and helping to pay the social security for his aging grandparents. He was followed by a brother named Chad, who is also an honor student at Washington & Lee, and their younger brother, Karl, who is still in high school in Farmville as I write this.

Tom and Nancy were next, and their first daughter is Brittany, presently a student at Bucknell, following in her parent's footsteps. Their second daughter is Devon, getting ready for college, and their youngest, Meredith is ready for high school at Quaker Valley, where Tom is a member of the school board.

Susan and Dan emulated Barb and Niels by having three sons. They attend the Fox Chapel schools. Wesley is now a student at Washington University in St. Louis, Kirk is getting ready for college, and Andrew has a few more years before that big event.

Laura and Chris were the last to get married, and they also have three children. Laura likes to point out to her brother and sisters that she was the only one to get it right: she has both daughters and a son: Emily, in high school, (Peters Township); Tom, just entering high school, and our youngest grandchild, little Julia, who seems to be getting taller every day.

I wouldn't want to create the impression that we are the typical doting grandparents. Speaking quite objectively, I must say that they are the most handsome, beautiful, intelligent and loving individuals I have had the good pleasure to meet. Their autobiographies will not be of ordinary lives!

So how did Quackers get into the title of this chapter? When the kids had gotten to the age that they didn't want to vacation with us, we started going to Cape Cod for summer vacations. Susan and Laura joined us in the early years, and we rented a house in Eastham. After a few years we settled on a house owned by Bob and Terry Chesney, which was near the beach on Cape Cod Bay. We enjoyed the house, but never got to meet the owners until one year we found them living in the house, Bob having retired. We enjoyed meeting them, but did not care for the house we rented that summer. With the urging of the kids, we started looking for a house to buy, and found a nice little Cape Cod house in Orleans. It was rather plain, and needed some landscaping to improve its appearance. So we bought it, with my law school classmate Fred Plumb representing the new buyers. It is located at 3 Black Duck Lane, and we felt this vast estate (one-half acre) deserved a name. I had been interested in the name of Winston Churchill's estate, called Chequers, and settled on a somewhat similar name: *"Quackers"*. So Quackers got a new face-lift with some landscaping and a screened-in porch. A few years later, we enlarged the garage and built a fourth bedroom above it, which became the "Captains Quarters", the occupants of which are Carlos and me.

I haven't told you about Carlos yet, but we had been thinking about getting a dog, and one day Ginnie was out walking along Black Duck and came across a man leading a handsome looking dog of an unfamiliar breed. He explained that she was a Portuguese Water Dog, a breed that does not shed and is compatible with any one claiming allergies, like me. And he said she had just had a litter of puppies and would she like to see them. When I got home that day, Ginnie told me she had found the puppy for us and took me to see the litter. Cute little waifs, so we put in our name to buy one of these. The breeder was most careful about who got these charmers, and we had to be interviewed and the pups had to be tested to see if our personalities matched up. Evidently they did, and we were awarded a pup that we named "Carlos", in honor of King Carlos of Portugal. The breeder liked our name, and Carlos was given the pedigree name *"Cutwater Summer Reign"*, the first part being the name of the breeding kennel, Summer because the pups were born on the summer solstice, and the last because he was named after a King.

I won't tax your patience by going on too much about Carlos, but it was a happy choice and he has been our constant and faithful companion for eleven years. He could have been a show dog (his sire won the Best of Breed at the Westminster Dog Show the year after we bought him) but we weren't interested in showing dogs, so our contract with the breeder required him to be neutered. The breed belongs with the working dog breeds, as they were used on Portuguese fishing boats for many years. They are intelligent, love to be with people, and Carlos is an accomplished kleptomaniac when it comes to food. He will steal anything he can reach, and does so at every unguarded moment. But we have spent more time laughing at him than swearing at him, and that's not a bad trade.

So Quackers has been our home for four or five months every year and we look forward to every return to that peaceful place.

30

Travels with Ginnie

We took vacation trips with the kids as they were growing up, and when they left the nest, Ginnie and I started to see the world on our own. Our first trip overseas was with a tour group from church, led by our then pastor, Richard Cromie, to England and Scotland. This was in July of 1974. We flew to Heathrow, and started off our tour at Windsor Castle. Proceeding north by bus, we visited Stratford-on-Avon, paid tribute to the bard, and proceeded on to Shrewsbury where we spent the night.

I still remember the feeling of excitement I felt on arriving in England. I had read books all my life about England and other countries, and here we were actually there! For a boy from Lawrence County, it was a thrill, and while visits to many other countries have been interesting and exciting, none has matched that first trip.

We proceeded by train to Edinburgh, and after touring that city, on by bus to St. Andrews. This was the real purpose of the trip for Richard, as he was submitting his doctoral thesis to his advisor at St. Andrews University. I went with him to his advisor's home, and was charmed by that erudite scholar. To make a memorable day of it, Richard and I then played a round of golf at the Old Course. After St. Andrews, Ginnie and I left the tour group for a few days and rented a car (first experience in driving on the left) and drove to Glasgow, and from thence flew out to Barra, the southernmost of the Outer Hebrides islands. The purpose of that was to visit our old friend, Ian MacNeil, my Ames partner at Harvard, who was now The MacNeil of Barra, succeeding to the title as Chief of the clan on the death of his father.

We flew out to Barra in a twin-engined Otter, and during the flight a lady next to me mentioned that we would be landing on the beach. I said that was a nice place for a runway, but she said "Oh, there's no runway, we just land on the beach." Sure enough, the airplane schedule varied each day with the tide, as the plane landed on the hard sand at low tide, after buzzing the beach to chase off the cows. It was a rather exciting landing, as the beach still had pools of water that we splashed through, but we eventually stopped and hopped out to meet Ian and his wife, Nancy. What a great day we had, and that night there was a dance held in honor of the Chief, and we found that Scottish square dancing made our American variety seem sedate by comparison.

The next day we flew back to Glasgow and took the train to Oban, where we rejoined our tour group. We traveled by bus up the west side of Scotland to Inverness, and circled around to the east side to Aberdeen, and eventually back to Edinburgh. At Culloden, after visiting the battle site, Richard and I got into a debate on the bus about the rights and wrongs of Bonnie Prince Charlie's campaign against England. Since Richard was stating the romantic Scot's view of it, I sided with the English view. The argument got so fierce that I had to buy him a dram of single-malt that evening just to make sure we remained friends.

We rented another car at Edinburgh and drove down through the Lake Country of England to London, and from thence home. We have enjoyed all of our adventures abroad, but none could beat that first voyage.

We made our first trip to Europe proper in 1977, when we took a trip through Germany, Austria and Switzerland with Bob and Jane Finley. Bob had been the Township Manager of Mt. Lebanon, and on his retirement took on the job of Office Manager for Buchanan Ingersoll. It was a great tour of the *Romantische Strasse*, Salzburg and the Alps in Austria and Switzerland. On the way back north, we visited daughter Susan at Freiburg, the real motive for the trip. She was taking a semester abroad in her junior year at Mt. Holyoke. We finished up the trip with a visit to the Armstrong ceilings plant in Munster, where we met Alex McNaugher, Armstrong's manager in Europe. The plant manager and assistant manager arranged a nice lunch for us. We got into a discussion about the war, when Alex had been in the Canadian RAF and bombing this part of Germany, and the managers had been on the receiving end. Herr Kalvilage, the Assistant Plant Manager and I had the discussion I mentioned earlier about our mutual but unfulfilled desire to get into the war.

In 1980, we traveled to Paris to meet daughter Susan again, and I have described that in an earlier chapter.

In 1982, Ginnie and I traveled on our own through Northern Italy, starting in Rome and proceeding to Florence, Venice and the Villa d'Este on Lake Como. My attempts to speak Italian usually ended up in Spanish, but the Italians are very forgiving and always encouraged me by pretending my Italian was quite good.

1984 took us to Egypt and a cruise down the Red Sea. We left Pittsburgh in a snowstorm, after several flights had been cancelled, but managed to get to New York just in time to catch up with our tour group. Our luggage, alas, was left somewhere in limbo. We finally managed to escape the storm in New York, but when we were about to arrive in Cairo, we were diverted to Athens because of a sandstorm in Egypt. We finally got there the next morning after a couple of hours of sleep in Athens, and got onto our cruise ship, with only the clothes on our backs. We sailed down the Red Sea and spent two days visiting Thebes, the Valley of Kings, and Karnak. After an afternoon hiking in the desert to a Roman quarry, our luggage miraculously caught up with us. We were ready for clean clothes. We crossed the Red Sea to the Gulf of Aqaba, and in Jordan visited the ancient rose red city of Petra, and drove down the valley of Lawrence's great attack in WW I. Back up the Red Sea to Cairo, and a grand tour of the Great pyramids at Giza as well as the more ancient pyramids at Memphis. A few days after we got home I came down with some malady involving chills and fever, but after several days in St. Clair Hospital, the doctors concluded it wasn't malaria, and I soon recovered.

The following year we traveled to Spain. We had talked to our friend, Nancy Miller, widow of my college classmate, Stat Miller, about joining us on the trip. She came to Pittsburgh around the New Year and we made our plans with the travel agent. In May, we got a letter from Nancy saying that she had been dating a man and would it be all right if he went on the trip also. We readily agreed, and put the travel agent back on the job of increasing our number. Our kids giggled about Mrs. Miller traveling with a man, but we told them to mind their manners. We met Fred Heller that summer, and were happy to have him join us. In August we got another letter from Nancy telling us they had decided to get married before the trip, and that this would be their honeymoon. I told Ginnie that not many people were invited to go on someone else's honeymoon, and that we were indeed privileged! What a honeymoon it was, and we greatly enjoyed the newly-weds and the trip to Madrid, Seville, Cordoba and the Mediterranean coast. We are still enjoying their company during our summers at Cape Cod.

In 1986, we set off with my brother, Willard and his wife, Florence, for a cruise around the Hawaiian Islands on the Constitution, a large cruise ship. Willard was always the life of the party, and we had a memorable two weeks with the California Pattons, visiting all the islands. It was the first time for Ginnie to spend some time with Willard and Florence, other than the brief visits we had to Los Angeles and their visits to the farm.

In 1987, I was invited to join a People-to-People trip to China. It was a large group of American lawyers and bankers led by Ed Meese, then the Attorney-General. We had several sessions discussing law with our Chinese counterparts, who were becoming interested in world trade, and knew they had to develop a legal system to handle it. There were also several large banquets in the Hall of the People, and a trip to see the Great Wall. I enjoyed meeting with bankers at the Bank of China, and the entrepreneurial types at CITIC, the Chinese organization that joined in partnerships with Western companies. We flew in and out of Hong Kong, so it was our first chance to visit that great city.

The same group, People-to-People, invited me on a similar trip to the Soviet Union in 1989. Gorbachev was in the final year of his reign, and change was in the air. The Russians were debating a new form of constitution and were eager to discuss their ideas with Americans. Little did any of us know that in a few months the change would bring down the Soviet Union and introduce a new regime for Russia. We had a great banquet at which Gorbachev spoke. We sat at a table with officials from Kazakhistan, and our problems with language were ameliorated by ample consumption of vodka. After the conference we traveled to Leningrad (before it became St. Petersburg again). While it was interesting, I was never happier to leave a country than when we flew back to Frankfurt, which seemed like home by comparison.

1993 marked my second retirement from Buchanan Ingersoll, and we celebrated by taking a five-week tour of New Zealand, Australia, Singapore and Hong Kong. In New Zealand we had the good fortune to meet Alan and Beryl Finch in Christchurch, and that friendship has led to several visits by the Finches to Pittsburgh and Cape Cod, and a return visit by us and our friends, Fred and Susan Plumb, to New Zealand in 2002.

1994 took us to Ireland, where I played golf with my regular foursome, while Ginnie stayed in Dublin at the home of Chris Norton's uncle. We rejoined her there and the two of us traveled around the Emerald Isle by car. 1996 included a grand trip around Alaska with Dave and Sally Keller, friends of ours from Southminster.

1997 took us on a Harvard cruise tour of the Baltics, with stops in Helsinki, St. Petersburg, the capitals of the three Baltic states, Kaliningrad (a Soviet disaster), Poland, Berlin and Copenhagen.

In 2000, I found that I could complete my continuing legal education requirements for the year by studying at Cambridge University. Ginnie and I lived at Emanuel College for one week, and following the Cambridge experience we drove over to Bristol for a visit with my former secretary, Annette Walker. From thence we drove to Cornwall and Devon, and saw much of that part of England.

We have had several trips to the Caribbean, with a number of visits to Cat Cay and our friends, Carl and Kay Doverspike. We also spent several days in 2001 in St. John in the American Virgin Islands.

Writing about these trips brings back a flood of happy memories, and I would write even more about each of them, but this tome is too lengthy as it is. Stop by sometime and I will regale you with more stories and my photos.

31

Retirement

I consider myself something of an expert on this subject as I have retired so many times. From the law firm in 1983, from the bank in 1990, from the firm again in 1992, from the two boards of directors in 1996, and from various non-profit agencies during this period. I still have a few things to retire from, such as serving as an arbitrator for the New York Stock Exchange and the NASD. I probably should retire from singing, and I have tried that but missed it so much I still turn up in church choirs at Southminster and Federated Church in Orleans.

So what does this great expert have to tell you about retirement? In a word, it's wonderful. For the first time in life, one is able to pursue one's own interests, without following someone else's schedule. In short, you are "free" and for an independent sort like me, that's great. So what do you do? Let me suggest some areas of interest.

Friends and Family. As grandparents, we dote on our twelve wonderful grandkids and never miss a graduation, a school play, a family dinner or whatever. Ginnie is even better at this than I, as she takes each grandchild out to lunch or dinner once each year, one-on-one. Since daughter Barbara lives in Virginia, we don't get to see her family as often as the other kids who live near us. But they often come to the Cape when we are there and we have seen a lot of their boys as they have grown up.

Tom and Nancy and their three daughters live in Sewickley, Susan and Dan and their three boys live in Fox Chapel, and Laura and Chris and their family in Peters Township, Washington County, a few miles south of us. I should add that we sold our house in Mt. Lebanon in 2003, and moved to a condominium in Upper St. Clair Township in a community called Hastings Village.

We like to get the whole family together, and usually the only time this is possible is Christmas, when the K's come to Pittsburgh and we celebrate the holiday in one or another family house. On our 40th wedding anniversary, the kids took us for a surprise weekend to the Southminster church camp in the wilds of Greene County, and on our 50th, we all went on a windjammer cruise out of Maine. What wonderful memories from all these events!

About ten years ago we decided to set up a family partnership, and put our securities and the house in Orleans in it as assets. Then we gave away partnership interests to the kids, and a few years later to the grandchildren, with their mothers as guardians. The object was to get them interested in investing, and thinking about retirement for themselves. It is never too soon to start planning for that. It also solved some estate tax problems for Ginnie and me, and the partnership has done well in that period of time. We have an annual meeting shortly after Christmas when everyone is here. We may not be wealthy, but we are unusually rich in family.

We have also have had our lives enriched with friends. We stay in touch with my contemporaries at Buchanan Ingersoll, most of whom still survive. It is always a pleasure to have dinner, lunch or just a drink with the Parks, Mortons, Armstrongs, and McLeans, to name a few. Jean McLean, known to her husband as the Queen Bee, asks that if Hollywood makes a movie of this book, she would like to be filmed in the bathtub, drinking a martini. Filmmakers, please note. Many old friends from my banking years are still here, so I get to see them from time to time. Pat Drury, my secretary/assistant from the law firm and the bank, has now retired from the bank and we get to play golf occasionally. John Echement and Bill Walker still keep an eye on me to make sure I don't get into trouble, and we have enjoyed New Years Day dinners with Bill and Linda Roemer.

We became Associate Members in the Federated Church of Orleans, and have found a number of new friends there, many associated with the choir: Dave and Pat Schoeffel (I have sung some duets with Pat), Bill and Jackie Stowell, and our ministers, Michelle Rogers-Brigham and Gordon Major. Our Cape Cod neighbors have also been a source of friends. At a party at our neighbor Ann Franklin's home, we met Allen and Barbara Riley, and Allen talked me into joining the Kings Way Golf Club, of which he was a member. We had several years of commuting together to the Club, with breakfasts at Grumpy's, and we have remained good friends even after they moved to Sandwich. Allen even came to Pittsburgh to cheer for the New England Patriots when they played the Steelers (and lost). Kings Way has also yielded up some friends who can tolerate my golf, such as Donna Hirshberg, and our neighbors, Dwight and Alice Wilson. I have enjoyed commuting to the golf course in Dwight's vintage pick-up truck, and they have shared their condo on Beacon Hill in Boston with us.

The years on the Westminster Board have left us with many close ties. There is a group of emeritus trustees who meet occasionally for lunch at the Duquesne Club that includes my long-time investment advisor Dave Hunter, my classmate Don Wiley, Bishop Donald Wuerl, and my old friend from banking days, Stan Gumberg. Both Stan and his wife, Marcia, have been long-time friends, along with their three fine sons, Ira, Larry and Andrew, and they all continue to prosper in various real estate ventures.

One of those Westminster friends is Scott Beck. I mentioned earlier that Oscar Remick and I had served on his company's board of directors. Scott is one of the most talented young entrepreneurs that I have met. Because of client confidentiality, I cannot discuss his current business operations, but I can say it has been a pleasure to get to know his father, Larry, and his brother, Tom, in that connection. Scott lives with his talented wife, Theresa, and their four charming daughters in Boulder, Colorado (when they aren't learning Spanish in Mexico) and we enjoy hearing from them frequently.

My colleagues in the Allegheny County Bar are too numerous to mention, but one Cookie Miller, a/k/a Willis McCook Miller, Jr. has been a constant source of encouragement in the writing of these memoirs, and I thank him for his prodding to finish this opus.

There are some consequences to living long, and not all of them are pleasant. One has to deal with deaths of family and friends, for example. My Dad died in 1981, leaving my mother living alone in their home near New Castle. I did my best to look after her and she was able to stay in her home until she was 99 years old. She needed to have a live-in companion the last few years, but eventually she fell and broke her hip, and efforts to mend it weren't successful. She eventually agreed to move to Asbury Heights near us, and we could visit almost daily. We then sold her house in Lawrence County. She lived for several more years, dying shortly before her 103d birthday. She is now buried in Neshannock cemetery, next to Dad.

Willard predeceased my Mother, so once again I had to be the bearer of bad news to her. He came down with the flu in December 1998, which developed into pneumonia, and despite every effort in the California hospital to save him, he didn't make it. When it appeared that he wasn't going to recover, Florence called us and Ginnie and I flew out to California and spent his last day at the hospital with him. I was able to talk to him, and he recognized me and squeezed my hand. He tried to answer, but he was in an oxygen tent and I couldn't understand what he was trying to say. I believe what he was saying was "Get me out of here." He didn't want to die in a hospital, and the following day he was sent home in an ambulance. He died the following morning. We held a memorial service later at Asbury, attended by Mother and our family.

Another dear friend was lost when Rosemary Plesset died in 2001. She had moved from Pittsburgh to Cape Cod where we saw her often during our stays at Quackers. She was diagnosed with lymphoma, and I drove her into Boston a few times to visit her oncologist. She endured the radiation and chemotherapy without complaint, but that did little but postpone what seems to have been inevitable. I had returned from a trip just before the 4th of July weekend and found that Ginnie had taken her to Cape Cod Hospital for a second round of chemotherapy. I went to the hospital to take her home, and she was happily looking forward to a visit from her son and family that weekend. She was also cheerfully planning on going on a skiing trip to Italy the next winter with her Over Seventy Ski Club.

The following day I returned from an afternoon boating to be greeted by Ginnie with the shocking news that Rosemary's family had arrived to find her dead in bed, with a book she had been reading beside her. It was unexpected and shattering news, as I loved her, Ginnie loved her and Carlos adored her. Of the three friends I would most like to meet in the hereafter or in some other universe, I list Glenn, Oscar and Rosemary. I have so much to tell them and they have more to tell me.

To finish these morbid tales, my brother, Gaylord died about a year after Mom's death. Like Willard, he had developed diabetes and eventually his kidneys failed him. Both had been heavy smokers, and I blame their deaths at the age of 70 on that. Both were cremated, and their ashes buried in the family plot at Neshannock.

Travel and Leisure: I have written about our travels, some of which occurred after retirement. That is certainly one of the pleasures of this time: the feeling that one can pick up and go somewhere else on short notice is a kind of freedom. Leisure also gives one lots of opportunities to do the things that are financially unproductive but quite enjoyable. I have enjoyed reading all my life, and now there is more time for that. The New York Times crossword puzzles are a great time-waster, but fun. Likewise roaming around on the internet, and all the hobbies one can tolerate. Education is a lifetime vocation, and retirement provides the time to do more of that. For example, I can now study quantum mechanics (even if the math is beyond my ken), and I am taking a computer course on calculus, which I didn't understand when I was 17 years old. I need not elaborate on all of this. My point is that you should enjoy whatever period of life you may be experiencing: it won't last forever. And one final thought: if you have missed some great adventure in your life, it's may not be too important. An ordinary life can be very good.

Epilogue

I do not know of a good way to end this opus, but I cannot do so without mentioning a dramatic change in our lives that occurred in August 2005. Ginnie was diagnosed as having ovarian cancer. After extensive surgery, she is undergoing chemotherapy as I write this and is progressing well. We live in hope, sustained by the support and prayers of family and an untold number of friends. I must express our gratitude for the pastoral care we have received during this time from Carol Seaman and John Mehl, our pastors at Southminster. We are grateful for the life we have enjoyed together, and will continue to enjoy every additional day we are granted.

At this point in an autobiography, one may be expected to pass on to the reader some gems of wisdom from the aging philosopher-author. I cannot do that, not because I have not learned anything from the life described, but because such advice is inevitably banal. You will learn to respect the ancient virtues from your life experiences, and not from any sermon I might deliver on that subject. To our grandchildren and their future descendants, I can only say that our prayers for your future lives will continue.

978-0-595-38598-0
0-595-38598-2

Printed in the United States
55382LVS00005B/397-411

9 780595 385980